Volleyball

Other titles in the Science Behind Sports series:

Volleyball

MELISSA ABRAMOVITZ

LUCENT BOOKS

A part of Gale, Cengage Learning

GALE
CENGAGE Learning·

Detroit • New York • San Francisco • New Haven, Conn • Waterville, Maine • London

LIBRARY OF CONGRESS CATALOGING-IN-PUBLICATION DATA

Abramovitz, Melissa, 1954-
Volleyball / by Melissa Abramovitz.
    pages cm. -- (Science behind sports)
Includes bibliographical references and index.
ISBN 978-1-4205-1157-4 (hardcover)
1. Volleyball--Juvenile literature. I. Title.
GV1015.34.A37 2013
796.325--dc23

2013001845

Lucent Books
27500 Drake Rd
Farmington Hills MI 48331

ISBN-13: 978-1-4205-1157-4
ISBN-10: 1-4205-1157-2

Printed in the United States of America

1 2 3 4 5 6 7 17 16 15 14 13

TABLE OF CONTENTS

FOREWORD

On March 21, 1970, Slovenian ski jumper Vinko Bogataj took a terrible fall while competing at the Ski-flying World Championships in Oberstdorf, West Germany. Bogataj's pinwheeling crash was caught on tape by an ABC *Wide World of Sports* film crew and eventually became synonymous with "the agony of defeat" in competitive sporting. While many viewers were transfixed by the severity of Bogataj's accident, most were not aware of the biomechanical and environmental elements behind the skier's fall—heavy snow and wind conditions that made the ramp too fast and Bogataj's inability to maintain his center of gravity and slow himself down. Bogataj's accident illustrates that, no matter how mentally and physically prepared an athlete may be, scientific principles—such as momentum, gravity, friction, and aerodynamics—always have an impact on performance.

Lucent Book's Science Behind Sports series explores these and many more scientific principles behind some of the most popular team and individual sports, including baseball, hockey, gymnastics, wrestling, swimming, and skiing. Each volume in the series focuses on one sport or group of related sports. The volumes open with a brief look at the featured sport's origins, history and changes, then move on to cover the biomechanics and physiology of playing, related health and medical concerns, and the causes and treatment of sports-related injuries.

In addition to learning about the arc behind a curve ball, the impact of centripetal force on a figure skater, or how water buoyancy helps swimmers, Science Behind Sports readers will also learn how exercise, training, warming up, and diet and nutrition directly relate to peak performance and enjoyment of the sport. Volumes may also cover why certain sports are popular, how sports function in the business world, and which hot sporting issues—sports doping and cheating, for example—are in the news.

Basic physical science concepts, such as acceleration, kinetics, torque, and velocity, are explained in an engaging and accessible manner. The full-color text is augmented by fact boxes, sidebars, photos, and detailed diagrams, charts and graphs. In addition, a subject-specific glossary, bibliography and index provide further tools for researching the sports and concepts discussed throughout Science Behind Sports.

CHAPTER 1

A Wildly Popular Sport

Volleyball is one of the most popular competitive and recreational sports in the world. More people participate in volleyball than in any other sport except soccer. Over 800 million people worldwide and 46 million Americans play volleyball professionally, competitively in school or in a league, and for fun. According to USA Volleyball, the governing body for volleyball in the United States, volleyball "is a lifetime sport enjoyed by players from [ages] 8 to 80. Participation in volleyball is not only good exercise, but also involves team competition and spirit."[1]

As popular as volleyball is today, it took many years for it to achieve its status as a favorite sport, and although volleyball was officially invented in the United States in 1895, it initially caught on faster in many other countries. It was not until after the exciting 1984 Olympics that volleyball became the wildly popular sport it is today in the United States.

Early Volleyball

Even before volleyball existed, people played ball games that contained volleyball-like moves, such as jumping to hit a ball and passing and hitting a ball around in the air. One of the first-known mentions of such a ball game appears in the epic poem, *Odyssey* (800 B.C.), written by Homer. According to the

Original Ideas Remain

Although many of the early volleyball rules changed after the first handbook was written in 1897, several important original practices remain a part of the game. One is the emphasis on playing as a team while still covering one's individual space on the court. The handbook of 1897 instructs, "Play together; cover your own space. Pass to one another when possible."

Another practice that remains is a requirement for good sportsmanship and respect for referees. The handbook states, "Any player, except the captain, addressing the umpire or casting any slurring remarks at him or any players on the other side, may be disqualified, and his side be compelled to play the game without him or a substitute, or forfeit the same." Similar regulations exist today.

Quoted in Byron Shewman. *Volleyball Centennial.* Indianapolis, IN: Masters Press, 1995, p. 3.

poem, two young men, during after-dinner entertainment at King Alcinous's court, "took up a beautiful purple ball which the craftsman Polybus had made for them. One of them, bending backwards, kept throwing it up towards the cloudy heavens; the other, leaping up, would catch it easily before his feet touched the ground again. When they had given proof of their skill with the high-thrown ball, they danced on the generous earth, passing the ball quickly to one another."[2]

Similar mentions of ball games that used an airborne ball appear in other ancient literature and history books, but it was not until 1895 that William Morgan, physical education director at the Mount Holyoke, Massachusetts, YMCA, formalized the sport he initially called mintonette. Morgan realized that the newly popular sport of basketball was too strenuous for the many middle-aged businessmen enrolled in his classes, and he decided to invent a new game that would provide exercise and be enjoyable without requiring as much running and physical contact as basketball did.

Morgan considered many possibilities, remarking, In search of an appropriate game, tennis occurred to me, but this required rackets, balls, a net and other equipment, so it was eliminated—but the idea of a net seemed a good one. We raised it to a height of about 6 feet 6 inches from the ground, just above the head of an average man. We needed a ball, and among those we tried was a basketball bladder, but this was too light and too slow, we therefore tried the basketball itself, which was too big and too heavy.[3]

Mintonette

Morgan ended up splicing together elements from several other sports to create mintonette. He derived the name from badminton, which uses a raised net and involves keeping a shuttlecock airborne. From baseball Morgan took the idea of allowing three strikes per hitter and three serves per team in each inning of mintonette. He also designed the game to last

A group of women play volleyball outdoors in the early 1900s, not long after YMCA physical education director William Morgan invented the game in Mount Holyoke, Massachusetts.

nine innings like baseball. From basketball he borrowed the idea of dribbling the ball, only in mintonette the dribbling took place in the air rather than on the ground. The players were also allowed to dribble to themselves behind a line 4 feet (1.2m) from the net called the dribbling line.

From handball Morgan borrowed the concept of allowing the ball to be played off surrounding walls, and from tennis he decided to allow each server two tries to complete a serve. Morgan also derived some inspiration from the European sport of faustball, also called fistball, which has been played for centuries. In fistball, players hit a ball with the fists or arms over a net and try to prevent opponents from returning the ball, much like in volleyball. However, in fistball the ball is allowed to bounce off the floor, and the court is larger than in volleyball.

Since the balls used in these other sports were not right for mintonette, Morgan asked sports equipment manufacturer A.G. Spalding to design a special ball. It created one with a leather and canvas cover, 25 to 27 inches (64 to 69 cm) around, weighing 9 to 12 ounces (255 to 340 g), with an exterior air valve and laces. It was similar to modern volleyballs, except modern ones have inside valves and laces to make them better balanced and less painful to hit. Modern balls are approximately 26 inches (66cm) around and weigh 9 to 10 ounces (255 to 283 g).

Morgan's new game made its competitive debut at Springfield College in Massachusetts on July 7, 1896. After this game, Springfield College faculty member A.T. Halstead suggested that the name of the sport be changed to volley ball, noting that volleying the ball back and forth across the net was its most prominent feature. Morgan agreed to the change. The sport was known as volley ball (two words) until 1952, when the name became one word.

The Need for Change

The rules for the new sport were first written down in a volleyball handbook published in 1897. Many of these rules changed drastically over the years, in large part because they were often vague and led to chaos on the court. These ongoing changes made many people reluctant to participate in or watch volleyball for many years. In their book, *Volleyball: Steps to Success*, coaches Bonnie Kenny and Cindy Gregory write, "Throughout its development, volleyball experienced the biggest drawback to its popularity because of frequent rule changes. Coaches had difficulty teaching volleyball because every few years the rules changed."[4]

THE 5-1 FORMATION

In modern volleyball games there are six players on the court for each team. There are a number of formations that these players can take, but the most common is the 5-1 formation, which means that there is one setter and five hitters on the court.

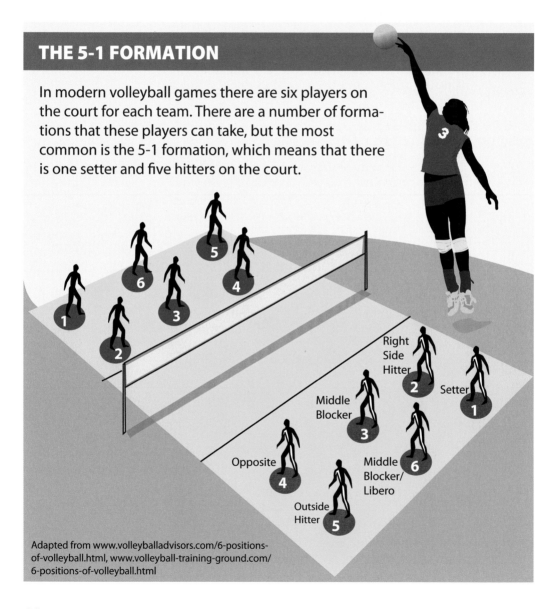

Adapted from www.volleyballadvisors.com/6-positions-of-volleyball.html, www.volleyball-training-ground.com/6-positions-of-volleyball.html

The Court

The dimensions of the volleyball court influence the science of the sport by determining where and how much players and the ball move. The first courts were 40 feet (12m) by 80 feet (24m). Since the early rules allowed an unlimited number of players on each team, the court was often crowded. However, when six players per team became the rule, the court was too big for each player to comfortably cover his area. Volleyball governing agencies, such as the Fédération Internationale de Volleyball (FIVB), therefore ruled that indoor courts would be changed to 30 feet (9m) by 60 feet (18m). Beach courts are generally 26 feet (8m) by 52 feet (16m) because competitive beach volleyball is played by two people per team. According to FIVB, "the entire 64 square meters of sand is shared by only two players, so teams tend to divide the court evenly and specialise in playing left or right."

Fédération Internationale de Volleyball. "The Game—Beach Volleyball." Fédération Internationale de Volleyball. www.fivb.org/thegame/TheGame_BeachVolleyball.htm.

Among the most contentious of the original rules was that there was no limit on the number of players on a team. Thus, having twenty or more players on the court at one time was not uncommon, which could be chaotic and confusing. There was also no limit on the number of times a person or team could touch the ball on each rally (back-and-forth play), so passing or dribbling the ball around could go on for hours. With nine innings in the original game, this could result in very long games. Rule changes were made gradually, and early volleyball leagues and rules committees throughout the world contributed their input on these changes as the sport began to spread to countries such as Canada, Cuba, Brazil, and the Philippines in the early 1900s. In his book, *Volleyball Centennial*, author Byron Shewman describes one match in the Philippines where "one team set the ball back and forth between themselves 52 times before hitting it over the net, the local rules committee observing the game demanded the first three-hit rule."[5] In the rules today each team is allowed to touch or hit the ball three times before sending it over the net.

Other early changes included removing the dribbling line from the court, standardizing the size of the court and the height of the net, allowing only six players per team on the court at one time, requiring either twenty-one or fifteen points to win a game (depending on the league), and changing the length of the game from nine innings to a match. The points and match requirements were later changed several times. The last time was in 1999 when the Fédération Internationale de Volleyball (FIVB), the organization that governs international volleyball, adopted rally scoring.

Before rally scoring was implemented, only the team that served the ball could score a point. When the receiving team won a rally, they only gained the right to serve. This was known as side-out scoring. Under rally scoring either team can win a point during a rally, and a match consists of one team winning at least three of the five games. The first four games are played to twenty-five points and the fifth to fifteen. Each game must be won by at least two points. By 2005, all competitive volleyball associations, including those that govern high school and college volleyball, had adopted rally scoring.

The FIVB cites several reasons for switching to rally scoring: "It will shorten long matches and add excitement, it maintains the basic structure of the game, provides chances for catch-up, is easy to understand and applicable to all ages and categories."[6] During a test phase of rally scoring, volleyball governing bodies in many countries found increased spectator interest and enthusiasm for the sport and less confusion over the scoring system.

Adding Excitement

In addition to confusing and rapidly changing rules, another factor that limited volleyball's appeal for many years was its reputation as a boring, unathletic sport for middle-aged

The libero for Oakland University's women's volleyball team gets into position to bump the ball in an intercollegiate match. The creation of the defense-minded libero position in the 1990s is one of several changes made to the game of volleyball over the years.

men. However, the introduction of volleyball into fiercely competitive collegiate and professional leagues and the Olympic Games as well as the development of new tactical innovations over the years gradually banished these perceptions as it became apparent that volleyball was an exciting, fast-moving, athletically challenging sport that required both power and finesse.

One of the earliest tactical innovations that added challenge and excitement was the set and spike technique, in which a ball that is high in the air is passed to a teammate who then spikes it hard and fast into the opponents' court. A Filipino team first used this move in 1916. Team members called it the "bomba," meaning kill, and called the hitter the "bomberino." Trying to return a kill is one of the most challenging skills in the sport, and the set and spike remains a central strategy for any team.

In the 1920s the act of blocking the ball at the net, rather than simply passing it around, became another accepted move, as did using an overhand serve rather than an underhand one. In the 1940s forearm passes, or bumps, became allowable, and in the 1960s defensive diving to the floor to get under the ball added even more challenge and excitement to the game. In the 1990s the libero, or defensive specialist, position was introduced, largely to give shorter players a chance to excel in volleyball. The libero is only allowed in the back row and wears a different jersey than his or her teammates. Adding the libero increased the level of expertise of defensive players and also increased volleyball's popularity by giving more people an opportunity to play in high-level competitions.

Schools to Pros

The changes in rules and tactics that made volleyball more exciting and athletically challenging also made it a more desirable sport for high school and college athletes. The YMCA, which sponsored most of the early tournaments and rule committees, worked hard to incorporate volleyball into school programs for many years, but progress was gradual. In 1916 the YMCA invited the National Collegiate Athletic Association (NCAA) to help revise the rules and to help promote volleyball in schools, but it took several decades before most colleges and high schools added volleyball. After the

Sailors at a naval base in Honolulu, Hawaii, play volleyball in 1945. The sport became popular among American military personnel during World War I.

U.S. Congress passed the Educational Amendments Act of 1972, which, in part, prohibits sex discrimination in schools, volleyball became especially popular among young women, and this helped boost its general popularity as people became aware that it could be a challenging sport for women as well as men.

Volleyball also received recognition as a tough sport from the military. During World War I (1914–1918), the U.S. War Department hired several YMCA physical education directors to bring volleyball to American soldiers as a fun recreational diversion. According to the Volleyball Hall of Fame, "because volleyball could be played by men of all ages, in a limited area, both in-or outdoors, the

SET AND SPIKE

Indoor volleyball first became an Olympic sport in 1957, and beach volleyball in 1992.

popularity of this sport among the U.S. Armed Forces was immense."[7] Over a million soldiers participated and grew to love volleyball, even sparking enthusiasm among their European colleagues. After World War I, the U.S. armed forces continued to promote and participate in recreational and competitive volleyball, and in 1952 the United States Volleyball Association added an armed forces program that brought teams into national tournaments and coaching clinics.

The greatest boost to volleyball's appeal came, however, after it became an Olympic sport in 1957. The first Olympic volleyball teams competed in the 1964 Olympics in Tokyo, Japan, and this helped increase public enthusiasm for both watching and playing the game in much of the world. In the United States an even bigger boost came when the U.S. men's team won the gold medal in the 1984 Olympics. The Volleyball Hall of Fame notes,

> The [1984] team did more than win this country's first Gold Medal [for volleyball], it captured the hearts of the American people and generated a new passion for the sport within the United States and around the world. Because of the team's success, more Americans began watching volleyball, playing volleyball, and enjoying volleyball. Volleyball players became heroes, and the sport born in the USA became "America's sport."[8]

Enthusiasm for professional volleyball spiked as well, particularly outside the United States in places like Italy, Japan, and Brazil. Many top American players went overseas, where they could earn a good living by joining professional indoor volleyball teams. Funding for American professional teams has been less successful, with the exception of professional beach volleyball tournaments.

Beach Volleyball

Beach volleyball got its official start after indoor volleyball did, but the beach game went professional and attracted many enthusiastic spectators long before the indoor game.

An aerial shot shows a crowd amassed around a volleyball court for a professional tournament in Hawaii, the state where the beach version of the game was introduced in 1915.

Beach volleyball officially started in Hawaii in 1915 when Outrigger Beach and Canoe Club swim coach George "Dad" Center set up a net and brought two volleyballs to the club's beach. The game initially gained many recreational players in Hawaii and Southern California, which is where it was mainly played for many years.

Beach teams have anywhere from two to six players per team (today, competitive teams have two), and in 1948 the first two-man beach tournament was held in Los Angeles,

California. The winners received a case of Pepsi as a prize. As the sport's popularity grew, the prizes improved. In the 1960s winners in tournaments in France received about thirty thousand francs (about $32,000). In 1979 winners in a Manhattan Beach, California, tournament received $11,000. Payouts for professional players today are much higher, and professional beach volleyball has a huge following and many sponsors.

In the 1950s beach volleyball became known in Southern California and Hawaii as much for its reputation as a party venue for toned, tanned athletes wearing skimpy bathing suits and drinking beer as it was for its athletic and recreational attributes. However, as more and more outstanding male and female athletes, including many top collegiate and nationally ranked players, began to participate, the public started to see beach volleyball as more of a fiercely competitive sport than merely a party sport. For female players, the sport's credibility gained momentum from the unbeatable team of Jean Brunicardi and Johnette Latreille in the 1960s. According to author Arthur R. Couvillon in his book, *The Sands of Time*,

> they were the first women who were able to spike the ball on the beach. This made the women's game more of an offensive minded game instead of just passing and shooting the ball all over the court. Prior to Brunicardi and Latreille's partnership, the women's game was mundane. People would only watch the game to see the attractive, healthy girls. . . . People started to watch the women's game for the competition rather than just for [the pretty girls].[9]

Thanks to outstanding male players like Gene Selznick and Ron Lang in the 1960s, men's beach volleyball also became known as an exciting, legitimate sport.

Volleyball Today

The legitimacy of beach volleyball as a truly competitive sport was cemented by its addition to the Olympics in 1992, and today both the beach and indoor versions command a huge worldwide following at all levels of play and competition. The modern game bears little resemblance to the chaotic, drawn-out game that characterized volleyball in 1895, but the changes over the years have helped volleyball become what William Morgan envisioned when he invented it—a fun, accessible sport for people of all ages.

CHAPTER 2

Physics and Volleyball

A s volleyball evolved over time, many of the changes related directly to the science behind the sport. For instance, the standardized size and weight of the ball and the size of the court were designed to accommodate the movements of the players, and these movements depend a great deal on how athletes interact with and control their physical environment.

Players' volleyball skills and their relationship to the court environment and the ball are mainly governed by the laws of physics and biomechanics. Physics is a science that describes and explains the properties and relationships between physical objects, and biomechanics is the study of how the laws of physics and mechanics affect how the human body moves. As the article "Sports Biomechanics: Physics of Sport" on the Topend Sports website states, "physics plays a dominant role in the way athletes perform and the way the sport is played."[10]

Forces of Nature

The laws of physics can be used to explain how forces control how the ball and the players move in volleyball. A force is simply a source of energy that pushes or pulls an object. Forces are measured in units called Newtons.

Several forces of nature are evident in the game of volleyball, such as the muscle activity that allows a player to jump; the contact force when he tosses and strikes the ball; and the gravity that affects the ball's path and his landing.

One Newton (N) equals the amount of total force needed to speed up something weighing 1 kilogram at a rate of 1 meter per second squared. That is, $N = kg \times m/s^2$, where kg = kilogram, m = meter, and s = second.

There are many forces at work in sports, including those generated by athletes' movements, the environmental and athlete-generated forces that act on a ball, and the forces applied to athletes by their surroundings. Author Miriam N.

Sir Isaac Newton

Sir Isaac Newton (1642–1727) was an English physicist and mathematician whose work provided the foundation for most of the modern physical sciences. His laws of motion explain the basic rules of physics that govern all sports, including volleyball. These laws apply to the motion of athletes and the ball and to the interactions of athletes and the ball with the court environment.

Born in Woolsthorpe, Lincolnshire, England, on December 25, 1642, Newton attended Cambridge University. When the university was temporarily closed due to a plague epidemic in 1665, Newton returned to his hometown and spent a great deal of time thinking about gravity and other physical and mathematical puzzles. It is rumored that he developed his ideas about gravity when an apple fell from a tree and hit his head, but historians are not sure whether or not this is true.

In 1667 Newton returned to school to complete his studies, and in 1669 he became a professor of mathematics. He made many contributions to science, including a reflecting telescope, and he conducted numerous experiments about gravity and about the composition of light. His most famous book, *Philosophiae Naturalis Principia Mathematica*, details how the force of gravity applies to the entire universe.

Satern explains some of these different forces in an article in the journal *Strategies: A Journal for Physical and Sport Educators*:

> Humans move from one place to another by applying a force against objects in their environment. To perform locomotion skills (e.g. walking, running, jumping, and skipping), humans apply force to the floor or ground. In sport, humans project objects (e.g. balls) by applying force to perform ballistic skills such as throwing, striking, and kicking. Conversely, humans absorb forces applied to different parts of their bodies when they perform manipulative skills such as catching and landing.[11]

The forces acting on volleyball players and volleyballs can be either internal or external, and multiple forces can simultaneously act on an object or person. Internal forces, created within an athlete's body, are generated by muscles, bones, and other body structures. External forces come from outside the object being acted on and can be applied through direct contact between objects or at a distance. An example of a contact force is the force placed on a volleyball by an athlete's moving hand. Forces that act at a distance, such as the force of gravity, which pulls objects to the earth's surface, are called field forces.

Newton's Laws of Motion

According to the laws of physics, if an object is at rest, the sum of the contact and field forces acting on it (the total force) is zero. Conversely, movement requires a force or forces to trigger this motion, and the total forces acting on a moving object determine the speed, distance, and direction it will travel. The main principles of physics that describe and explain how these forces influence each other are Newton's laws of motion, created in the mid-1600s by Sir Isaac Newton, an English physicist and mathematician. In an article on the LiveStrong.com website, A.G. Moody writes that Newton's "mathematical explanation for the way two objects interact, the three laws of motion, is the governing principle behind all sports, including volleyball."[12]

Newton's first law of motion states that an object at rest will stay at rest and an object in motion will stay in motion at the same speed and in the same direction unless an outside force acts to change its velocity. Velocity is a measurement of how fast an object is changing its original position. It is not the same as speed, since speed only measures how much distance something travels in a certain amount of time, while velocity measures speed plus direction.

Newton's first law features the principles of inertia and momentum. Inertia is the tendency of an object at rest to remain at rest. Inertia increases with the mass of the object—that is, more force is required to move a more massive object from a resting position. Mass is a measurement of how much matter an object contains. Unlike weight, which results from the force of gravity pushing on an object, mass does not depend on gravity. The mass of an object is the same on Earth as it is in a place that has no gravity, like Earth's moon.

Momentum is the opposite of inertia. Once a force puts an object in motion, momentum keeps the object in motion unless it is stopped by another force. An object's momentum equals its mass times its velocity. Thus, a more massive object has more momentum than a smaller, lighter object does, and more force is needed to stop or slow it.

Newton's second law of motion also involves inertia and momentum and explains how velocity changes when a force is applied to overcome an object's inertia. It states that the acceleration of an object (how much it speeds up) is directly proportional to the total external forces acting on it and inversely proportional to the object's mass. In other words, the more force that is put on an object, the faster it will speed up, but more massive objects do not accelerate as quickly as less massive ones do. If someone hits a volleyball and a basketball with the same force, for example, then the volleyball accelerates faster than the basketball because it has less mass.

Newton's third law addresses how the forces that act on objects interact. It states that every action creates an equally forceful and opposite reaction. This means that when a force, such as an athlete's moving hand hits a ball, the ball also applies an equal and opposite force to the hand. Another reaction force that plays a role in volleyball is the ground reaction force exerted by the floor on which an athlete's feet press. These reaction forces are in fact related to many sports injuries because they put stress on athletes' body parts.

Newton's Laws and Volleyball

Newton's laws apply to every aspect of volleyball, and volleyball players use these principles when practicing their skills and planning their game strategies. Athletes do not usually think about applying the laws of physics when they train or play a sport, but through experience they learn how these principles operate and how to best harness and control the applicable forces. Jeff Mitchell, a scientist at the Brookhaven National Laboratory who regularly play volleyball, says, "If I thought about volleyball's physics, I wouldn't be able to play

A defensive player's return of an incoming serve demonstrates Newton's third law, which states that the force of the incoming ball will generate an equal but opposite force when it hits the player's arms. The player can attempt to control that force by bending or moving his body to absorb it.

the game." Adds fellow player Travis Shrey, "You can't teach this [volleyball physics]. It's experience."[13]

Experienced players learn to harness the principles of physics in many ways. For instance, since a certain amount of force is required to overcome an object's inertia and provide momentum according to Newton's first law, volleyball players learn that they can transfer the momentum from a moving arm and shoulder to the ball to make it fly and that they can vary the amount of force to make it travel a certain distance. Transferring the momentum from other moving muscles, for instance, can increase the force to make the ball travel farther, as when an athlete recruits muscles in the legs to jump up while hitting the ball. In volleyball if the force applied is too great, then the ball will land outside the baseline. If it is too small, then the ball will not clear the net, so regulating the right amount of applied force is critical.

According to Newton's second law, which can be used to explain how the combination of internal and external forces affect the flight path of a ball, the more force a player puts into hitting the ball, the more the ball will accelerate and the farther it will travel. Since the mass of the ball is constant, its acceleration depends on how hard it is hit. The precise mass of a standard volleyball was in fact chosen to allow the greatest initial release velocity and subsequent acceleration when it is hit into the air with a maximum amount of force. A study at the Research Institute for Olympic Sports in Finland

Careers in Biomechanics

Biomechanics is a subdiscipline of kinesiology, the field of science that studies movement. Biomechanics focuses on studying how principles of physics and mechanics apply to body motions. A range of professionals, including athletic trainers, coaches, physical therapists, sports medicine experts, and laboratory researchers, work in careers related to biomechanics. These professionals conduct research to better understand human motion, design machines that help with athletic performance and mobility for people with various disabilities, and consult on sports training and sports medicine.

Most people who work in biomechanics have a strong background in math, physics, exercise physiology, and research. Most earn an undergraduate degree in kinesiology and then an advanced degree in engineering, biology or medicine.

shows, for example, that volleyballs have greater release velocities than more massive balls, such as soccer balls, when hit with the same force. The average release velocity of a volleyball hit by an elite player is close to 98 feet (30m) per second, while the average release velocity for a soccer ball is under 82 feet (25m) per second.

Newton's second law also applies to defensive situations. If an incoming ball is accelerating slowly, the player who receives it must apply more force to change its direction and make it land where he wants it to land than he would if it were accelerating quickly. This is because a slowly accelerating and slower-moving object has less momentum than one that is quickly accelerating and moving faster. The slower-moving object thus transfers less momentum when it collides with an athlete's hand, and the athlete must add more force to change the object's velocity.

The amount of acceleration, velocity, and force in a defensive situation is also governed by Newton's third law. When a defensive player blocks an incoming ball, he applies force to the ball and the ball applies an equal and opposite force to his hands or arms. A fast-moving ball's greater momentum generates a greater opposing reaction force, which causes the ball to rebound from the arms or hands with more force than a slower-moving ball would. To prevent the ball from rebounding with too much force, which could send it out-of-bounds, the athlete may have to bend her arms, legs, or torso to absorb some of the force.

Bending a body part absorbs force from a moving object because increasing the time and distance over which an object slows down decreases the force it exerts. This property of physics can be easily visualized by looking at the design of modern car bumpers. Engineers used to design rigid bumpers until they realized that in a collision, these bumpers quickly stopped the colliding object and the car's passengers were often severely injured by the incoming force. Modern bumpers are designed to crumple in a collision. This allows

SET AND SPIKE

Many volleyball players jump up to 300 times in a single match, generating huge amounts of force with their muscles.

them to absorb some of the incoming force by slowing down the reaction, thereby reducing the chances that passengers will be injured.

Ground Reaction Force

Newton's third law also explains the dynamics of the force exerted by a volleyball court on the players and the ball, known as the ground reaction force. When a moving ball

A beach volleyball player's feet sink into the sand while she awaits a shot. The sand creates a resistance of movement caused by friction, which means that beach volleyball players must exert more energy and effort in moving around the court than volleyball players on an indoor surface.

hits a hard court floor, the soft, less-massive ball applies less force to the floor than the floor applies to the ball, so the ball bounces to equalize the ground reaction force. In beach volleyball, the soft sand creates a ground reaction force closer to the force the ball exerts on the ground, so the ball bounces less, if at all.

The relationship between people and the ground reaction force is similar. When a person stands still on the ground, she exerts a force equal to her weight, and the ground exerts an equal and opposite force on the individual. When she moves, however, the ground reaction force changes because her feet press against the ground intermittently. The harder and faster her feet press against the ground, the greater the ground reaction force becomes. When she lands after running or jumping, a ground reaction force of more than twice her body weight can result. These increased forces cause stress on the muscles and joints that absorb the extra force, and this is why the ground reaction force is responsible for many sports injuries.

In beach volleyball the ground reaction force acting on an athlete differs from that on a hard floor, and while moving around in soft sand creates less ground reaction force, it poses other difficulties because sinking into sand adds resistance to movement. Running through a thick substance, such as sand, is more difficult than running through air because the friction exerted by sand on moving body parts is greater than that exerted by air. Friction is the force that decreases the movement of substances or objects sliding past each other. Scientists say it takes 1.6 times more energy to run in sand than on a hard surface. An article on the Strength and Power for Volleyball.com website states, "The quickest beach volleyball players run on top of the sand, they don't sink. If you are slow, you'll sink and it will end up taking more effort and energy to move. So really, if you move quick on top of the sand not only will you be quicker, you may actually conserve energy."[14]

Since many volleyball players participate in both indoor and beach volleyball, learning to accommodate the different ground reaction and resistance forces on each type of court can be challenging. Championship beach and indoor player Karch Kiraly says, "I guess the hardest thing is timing because you start moving a lot earlier [on the beach] to accomplish the same thing. It's even more drastic than going from the grass [tennis court] of Wimbledon to the clay [tennis court] of the French Open."[15]

Gravity and Spinning Volleyballs

In addition to the ground reaction force, there are a number of other physics principles that apply to external forces in volleyball. When hitting and receiving the ball, for instance, players must account for the force of gravity, which pulls the ball to Earth, causing it to descend from its flight path at some point after it is launched. Through experience, athletes learn how much force they must apply to the ball to either enhance or diminish the force of gravity. A ball hit higher into the air, for example, will stay aloft longer, but one hit too high will hit the gym ceiling and drop quickly.

The Surroundings Matter

Most of the time weather only affects the physics and biomechanics of outdoor volleyball. On rare occasions, however, indoor volleyball players may have to contend with weather-like factors. During the 1963 Pan-American Games in Brazil, the U.S. men's team could not figure out why most of their serves were not staying in bounds. Finally, one player noticed that before the Americans served, someone kept opening a large door at the back of the gym. Each time the door opened, the wind blew in affecting the serve. Although the team protested and asked game officials to ensure that the door remained closed, the officials refused. The U.S. team lost the match, and the team attributed the loss to that open door. The team was outraged by what it saw as the Brazilians' lack of fair play and by the referees' favoritism toward the Brazilians, but umpires' rulings are not up for discussion, fair or not.

FORCES AT WORK

When a player serves or returns a volleyball, there are many forces acting on it that have to be considered.

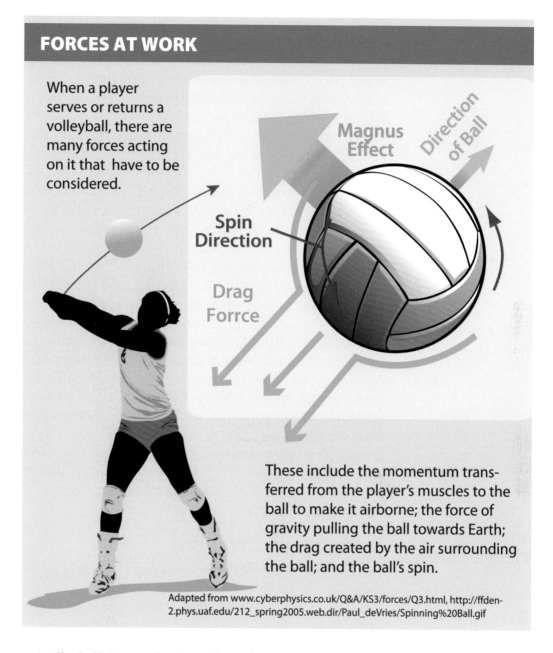

Magnus Effect

Direction of Ball

Spin Direction

Drag Forrce

These include the momentum transferred from the player's muscles to the ball to make it airborne; the force of gravity pulling the ball towards Earth; the drag created by the air surrounding the ball; and the ball's spin.

Adapted from www.cyberphysics.co.uk/Q&A/KS3/forces/Q3.html, http://ffden-2.phys.uaf.edu/212_spring2005.web.dir/Paul_deVries/Spinning%20Ball.gif

Volleyball players also learn that other factors, such as the amount of spin they put on the ball, affect the force of gravity. The effects of spin on an object's path are governed by a principle of physics called the Magnus effect, which states that a spinning object will change its path through the air according to the direction of the spin. Heinrich Gustav Magnus, a German chemist and physicist, demonstrated the principle that bears his name in 1852. Another principle called Bernoulli's principle, demonstrated by the Swiss mathematician Daniel Bernoulli in the 1700s, also applies to spin. Bernoulli's principle states that the faster the air moves over or around an object, the less pressure the air puts on the object.

The Magnus effect occurs because when an object, such as a ball, is not spinning, the pressure of the air moving around it is equal on all sides, but when spin is added, the spin changes this air pressure. Topspin, which volleyball players commonly add to a serve, causes the top of the ball to move in the direction opposite to that of the airflow around it, while the bottom of the ball moves in the same direction as the air does. The opposing motion on the ball's top creates drag, or increased air resistance on this part of the ball, and this drag makes the air move more slowly over the top and faster under the bottom. The slower-moving air puts more pressure on the ball than faster-moving air does, and this creates the Magnus effect that pushes the ball downward. According to a 2006 study, it is this "downward force due to the spin which makes the ball drop to the ground faster than it would with no spin."[16] Accelerating the rate at which the ball drops is desirable in volleyball, because it is more difficult for an opponent to hit a rapidly dropping ball. This is because the opponent has less time to judge where the ball is going to land and to move to that spot to intercept it.

Volleyball and Wobble

The effects of air pressure can be changed not only by the direction of the spin that is put on an object, but also by the characteristics of the object's surface. The surface of a volleyball is not smooth, as it contains small indentations between the patches that make up the ball. These indentations affect the air drag and therefore the motion of the ball.

Volleyball players often use the effects of the less-than-smooth ball to their advantage when performing a type of serve called a float. A float serve is an overhead serve that the athlete launches with a "punch" of the hand on the ball and a movement similar to that of shooting a bow

and arrow. It lacks spin, but it confuses opponents with an erratic, wobbling, and unpredictable flight path known as a lateral deviation or lateral deflection, similar to that seen in a baseball knuckleball pitch. This flight path results from the way air flows over the ball's indentations, causing what is called boundary layer asymmetry.

The boundary layer is a thin layer of air around an object. A less-than-smooth surface on a moving object will cause the air speed in this boundary layer to become irregular, which leads to varying amounts of pressure and drag on different parts of the object. These factors produce the object's lateral deviation, or sideways motion. A study by the National Aeronautics and Space Administration (NASA) on volleyballs found that the sideways motion in a float serve is greatest when the ball is slowing down and beginning to drop due to gravity. It states, "A serve that starts off on a straight flight path may suddenly develop a sideways motion towards the end of the flight."[17]

Special Effects in Beach Volleyball

In beach volleyball the movement of the ball is affected not only by gravity and the fairly stable air that surrounds it, but also by outdoor wind conditions. Players must be aware of

Kerri Walsh drops a handful of sand to check the direction of the wind before a beach volleyball match at the 2012 Olympic Games. The presence and direction of wind can affect the force with which a player hits the ball.

which way and how hard the wind is blowing to adjust the force with which they hit the ball. For example, if the wind is blowing into the athlete's face, this is called a headwind, and it adds resistance around the ball. Thus, the ball needs to be hit harder than if there was no wind, since more force is needed to make the ball travel the same distance. If the wind is blowing in the direction in which the ball will travel (a tailwind), then the player should apply less force and aim the ball to land less deep in the opponent's court than he normally would. For conditions where the wind is blowing across the court, "the trick is to serve into the wind, either short or deep. This will cause the ball to peel off or drop suddenly,"[18] explains Brain Lewis in an article in *Volleyball Magazine*. This happens because the wind slows the ball's forward motion and causes it to curve in the direction the wind is blowing.

All volleyball skills require athletes to harness and control various types of forces. As a result, training and conditioning programs for volleyball players include instruction and practice in how and when to use certain body parts to apply or absorb these forces.

CHAPTER 3

Physical Training

The laws of physics govern how volleyballs and volleyball players move and interact on the court, and competitive volleyball players use the laws during the training and skill drills to improve their performance. The ability to control the ball and perform the necessary skills depends on training various parts of the body to work in harmony with the laws of physics and biomechanics. Training sessions involve drills to teach and perfect each skill, along with the overall body conditioning and strengthening needed for athletes to play effectively and consistently throughout tiring matches.

Muscle Mojo

Volleyball skills and physical conditioning depend on building and coordinating the muscles that control movement. Humans have three types of muscles: smooth, cardiac, and skeletal. Smooth muscles are found in organs and blood vessels throughout the body, and like the cardiac muscle that allows the heart to pump blood, they operate involuntarily, without an individual's conscious control. The skeletal or striated muscles that control movement via their connections to bones (the skeleton), however, are under voluntary control.

All muscles are made up of elastic tissue that stretches and contracts, or shortens, to move various body parts. This

WORKING TOGETHER

There are a number of antagonist muscle pairs in the body that work together to create movement. When one muscle in a pair contracts (the agonist), the other one relaxes (the antagonist). Two of the most important muscle pairs for volleyball movements are the hamstrings/quadriceps pair and the biceps/triceps pair.

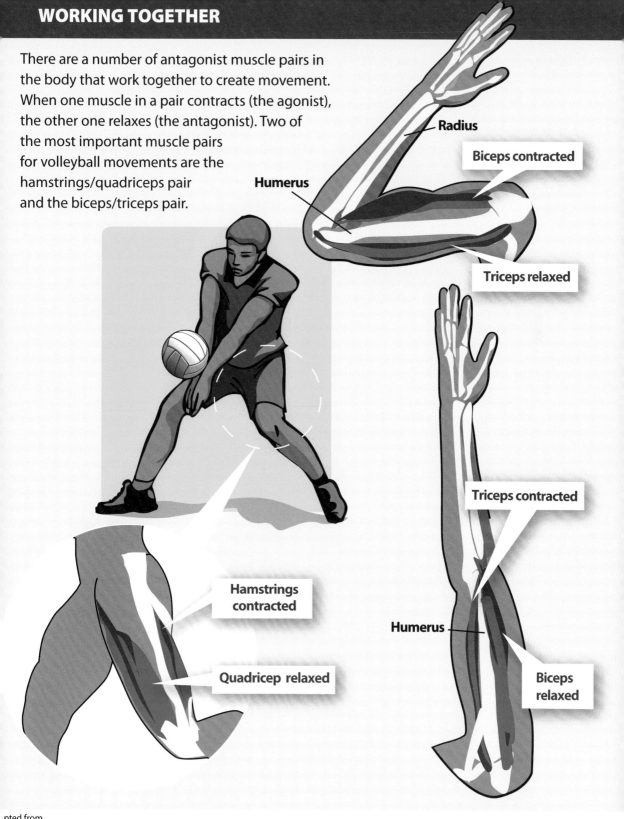

Radius

Humerus

Biceps contracted

Triceps relaxed

Triceps contracted

Humerus

Biceps relaxed

Hamstrings contracted

Quadricep relaxed

SET AND SPIKE

Playing volleyball works every major muscle group in the body and playing for 45 minutes burns about 585 calories.

tissue is made of cells called muscle fiber cells or simply muscle fibers. People have two main types of muscle fibers: slow twitch (ST) and fast twitch (FT). ST fibers contract more slowly than FT fibers do but tire less quickly. Since ST fibers burn oxygen for energy, they are most useful for aerobic or endurance exercise. FT fibers quickly burn oxygen as well as sugars and are best suited to creating the short bursts of speed and power needed in most volleyball skills.

Muscle fibers lengthen or contract in response to chemical and electrical signals from neurons (nerve cells) in the brain and spinal cord. When a person wants to move a body part, the brain sends messages to spinal motor neurons that control muscle fibers and muscles in a particular joint. In the elbow joint, for example, the applicable muscles are the biceps, brachialis, brachioradialis, and triceps in the arm. If an individual wishes to bend an elbow, motor neurons that control the biceps, brachialis, and brachioradialis start firing and instruct these muscles to pull on the tendons (cartilage that connects muscles to bone) and ligaments (cartilage that connects bones to each other) that connect to the humerus, radius, and ulna bones. This pulls the arm up at the elbow joint. To straighten the arm, the brain activates motor neurons that tell the triceps muscle on the back of the upper arm to contract, which pulls the forearm down. When activated by motor neurons in this manner, muscles provide the forces that allow the skeleton to move and to act on things in the environment.

The amount of force a muscle exerts depends in part on the number and the rate of firing of the motor neurons that control it. The more motor neurons that are involved and the faster they fire, the more force the muscle generates. Force also depends on the type of muscle fibers present and on the size of a muscle. FT fibers generate more force than ST fibers do. In an article on the CoachR.org website, kinesiology expert Jason R. Karp writes, "Although the type of fibers cannot be changed from one to another, training can change the amount of area taken up by the fiber type in the muscle."[19] Strength training exercises, such as lifting weights, cause FT fibers to get larger and ST fibers to get smaller, and aerobic exercises, such as jogging, do the opposite.

Building Muscles

Another method of increasing muscle forces is to enlarge the muscles. One way of doing this is to gradually overwork a muscle or muscle group using resistance or weights. This leads to small amounts of damage to muscle fibers. The body quickly repairs this damage over a few days, and this leaves the muscles slightly larger than they were before the damage. This growth occurs because damaged muscle fibers release chemicals called growth factors, and these chemicals cause satellite cells outside muscle fibers to fuse with the

Members of Russia's men's volleyball team work out in a weight room during a training session. Resistance training breaks down muscle fibers, which then repair themselves to an increased size and level of strength.

fibers. The chemicals also induce satellite cells to reproduce. This fusion and reproduction in turn trigger muscle fibers to produce more of the proteins actin and myosin, which are major components of muscle fibers. This adds to the muscle's size and also increases its strength. The strength is increased because the action of actin and myosin cells sliding past each other provides the force for muscle contractions. In an article for the Idea Health & Fitness Association, Karp explains, "The more actin and myosin proteins you have in your muscles, the more force they can produce. A boat with eight oars stroking the water is stronger and more powerful than a boat with two."[20]

Volleyball Training Takes Time

Developing the necessary skills for volleyball takes time. According to authors Bonnie Kenny and Cindy Gregory in their book, *Volleyball: Steps to Success*, "volleyball is a unique sport, one that takes years to master. Few of the skills … are natural movement patterns. How many times during your daily life does an object rebound off your forearms or do you run and jump to hit something while in the air?"[1]

Volleyball training also takes time because "each volleyball player must be efficient in executing all the required skills of the game if team success is to occur,"[2] according to Edward Spooner in his book, *The Science of Volleyball Practice Development*. In sports such as baseball and football, players train for their particular position on the team: pitchers train to pitch, outfielders train to catch and throw, and quarterbacks train to pass the ball. In volleyball, however, players do not specialize. They must train for every aspect of the game.

1. Bonnie Kenny and Cindy Gregory. *Volleyball: Steps to Success*. Champaign, IL: Human Kinetics, 2006, p. 149.
2. Edward Spooner. *The Science of Volleyball Practice Development and Drill Design*. Bloomington, IN: iUniverse, 2012, p. 2.

Another method of building muscle size and strength is through anaerobic exercises, such as short sprints. While longer runs build aerobic fitness and endurance, short sprints use up oxygen, and muscles must then break down carbohydrates, or sugars, for energy through a process called glycolysis. Glycolysis creates a chemical called lactic acid, which makes muscles larger and stronger. Lactic acid can also lead to muscle soreness, so athletes must be careful not to overdo any exercises that lead to its production. Trainers also say that having overly large muscles is a disadvantage in volleyball because muscle tissue is heavy and slows players down, so volleyball athletes limit the amount of muscle building exercises they do.

Muscle Energy

Besides helping to build muscle mass, glycolysis also creates adenosine triphosphate (ATP), which is the chemical that muscles use for the energy they need to generate the forces that move body parts. Once ATP is used for energy, more

A banana sits among bottles of water on the bench of Great Britain's men's volleyball team during the 2012 Olympics. In addition to physical training, athletes depend on proper nutrition and hydration to maintain energy.

SET AND SPIKE

A typical volleyball skill, such as a spike, takes between 5 and 30 seconds to execute.

energy is required for cells to manufacture more ATP. There are three types of chemical reactions that can provide this additional energy. In the first type, the body converts phosphocreatine, a chemical stored in muscle cells, into ATP. This process does not use oxygen and is thus an anaerobic chemical reaction. It can only be sustained for about ten seconds. For more prolonged energy production, muscle cells go back to using the anaerobic process of glycolysis. Glycolysis burns glucose or glycogen (glucose stored in the liver) to generate ATP, and this chemical reaction can be sustained for about two minutes. After this, if more energy is needed, the aerobic energy system, which takes oxygen from blood and burns both fat and sugars, produces most of the ATP.

The creation and use of energy by the human body is governed by a law of physics called the first law of thermodynamics, which states that energy cannot be created, but must be converted from one form to another. Muscle cells convert the nutrients they receive from a person's diet into the chemicals they need to create ATP and then convert this chemical energy to the kinetic energy (the energy of motion) they use to move. For this reason, athletes depend on good nutrition to give them the nutrients they need for this process.

According to nutritionists Robert J. Reber and Donald K. Layman, "without the right foods, even physical conditioning and expert coaching aren't enough to push you to your best. Good nutrition must be a key part of your training program if you are to succeed."[21] Athletes require a well-balanced diet to provide adequate protein, fats, and carbohydrates for optimal cell growth, maintenance, and energy production. They tend to need more carbohydrates than nonathletes do because they need stored glycogen, which is derived from carbohydrates, to convert to glucose during prolonged exertion. This is why many athletes eat carbohydrate-rich meals containing rice, pasta, whole grains, and vegetables before competitions. These types of complex carbohydrates (carbohydrates that are slowly digested) are the best types of carbohydrates for generating lasting muscle energy. Simple carbohydrates, however, such as sugar, cookies, candy, white bread, and some fruits, are digested quickly and provide only a quick burst of energy.

Carbohydrates are not the only nutrients essential to success as an athlete. Fats, found in foods like meats, dairy products, and vegetable oils, are also essential as a source of fuel that muscle cells and other cells can burn for energy. Proteins, the main nutrients found in meats, fish, eggs, nuts, and dairy products, are important for athletes too, as they

Training and Success

For many years American volleyball champions received little or no training or financial support from the United States Volleyball Association. In other countries, such as Russia, Cuba, and Japan, however, elite players trained year-round and received government or volleyball governing agency support, and this led to their national teams being virtually unbeatable. Until comprehensive training programs were organized in the United States in the 1970s, American teams did not succeed in winning in international competitions such as the Olympics.

One American player who advocated for well-funded, consistent training programs for Olympic volleyball athletes was Mary Jo Peppler of the 1964 U.S. women's Olympic team. Her team had only a two-week training camp before the Olympics that year, and it did not include any skills drills or team strategy sessions that could have helped the players perform better in competition. According to Peppler, it was a poorly organized waste of time that let the players know they were not valued. She says, "I remember two things said to me at that camp. 'Circle out!' which meant get in hitting position, and 'bend your knees more, honey.'"

Quoted in Byron Shewman. *Volleyball Centennial*. Indianapolis, IN: Masters Press, 1995, p. 104.

provide the amino acids (protein building blocks) needed to repair muscles and other body tissues. Another important element of good sports nutrition is adequate water intake. Without enough water the body can overheat and dehydrate, which can be fatal.

Training and Physics

While good nutrition is essential for top athletic performance, it cannot enhance performance by itself. Also needed are ongoing training and conditioning sessions to maximize muscle energy production and muscle function. Since most volleyball skills require short, intense bursts of energy, many training drills seek to enhance anaerobic energy production. However, training also includes drills to improve aerobic energy production to give athletes the endurance to function well during long matches.

Volleyball skills that make the most of biomechanics and players' physical interactions with the environment rely on muscles throughout the body, and training programs

Members of China's women's volleyball team partner up for a balance exercise during a training session.

seek to enhance speed, quickness, balance, coordination, strength, power, agility, and flexibility in all these muscles. For instance, coordination allows an athlete to regulate the amount of force she puts into jumping, hitting the ball, or other skills by integrating these skills with sensory information from the environment. In serving, for example, the player's eyes receive information about the ball's position after it is tossed upward, and the brain coordinates this information with instructions about when to contact the ball and how much force to put into jumping up and swinging the arm.

Other qualities, such as quickness, depend on coordination as well. Quickness is often confused with speed, but speed just involves how far someone or something moves in a given amount of time. Quickness refers to how fast someone reacts to whatever is going on around him and starts moving. It also refers to how fast the person stops after a burst of speed. Quickness requires even more control over the forces put out by the muscles than speed does because it includes coordinating one's reactions to events with moving quickly.

Closely related to quickness is agility, or the ability to move the body quickly in any direction. Flexibility, or range of motion, which is the distance someone can move a muscle without pain, is similar to agility, but differs in that flexibility does not include the element of quickness. Flexibility and agility depend on age (younger peoples' muscles tend to be more flexible and agile than older peoples' muscles), gender (females tend to be more flexible than males), how much an individual's muscles are regularly stretched and conditioned, and on muscle size. Large muscles are less flexible and agile than smaller ones are, in part because more massive objects have more inertia than less massive ones do.

Strength and Power

The other important qualities volleyball players seek to develop are strength and power. Strength refers to the amount of force someone is capable of applying, while "power is work per time. That is, if you do the same amount of work in a shorter time, it takes more power,"[22] according to the UCLA (University of California, Los Angeles) Physics & Astronomy

K-6 Connection website. The physics equation that describes power is called the force-velocity relationship. It states that power equals force times distance, divided by time.

One important determinant of muscle power is muscle fiber type. "Muscles with predominantly more [FT fibers] will produce more power than muscles with predominantly [ST fibers],"[23] states the National Council on Strength & Fitness. This is because FT fibers generate more ATP than ST fibers do.

Power also depends on the angular velocity of a muscle or joint. Angular velocity is a measurement of how fast an object is rotating. The relationship between power and the angular velocity of a muscle is complex. According to the National Council on Strength & Fitness, "muscle power is lowest at both very slow and very fast speeds. The peak power region generally occurs at approximately 40–60% of maximum angular velocity of the muscle."[24] Athletes thus train themselves to produce the most power by regulating how fast their muscles and joints move.

A Training Workout

Different types of training and conditioning exercises and drills help athletes develop different qualities, such as power and agility. Volleyball practice sessions start with warm-ups to get the nervous system and muscles ready for action. Common warm-ups are leg and arm swings, squats, push-ups, and slow jogging. After warm-ups, stretching the muscles is important for increasing flexibility and preventing injuries and soreness. A training workout usually includes static stretches (stretching while holding a position) and dynamic stretches (stretching muscles while gently moving them, perhaps with an elastic band).

After warm-ups and stretching, exercises to enhance balance, strength, quickness, and power are performed. Balance exercises involve keeping the head level when the rest of the body changes position and keeping the body weight evenly distributed over the feet. Holding one leg elevated and rotating it while standing is one method of improving balance. Another is moving while staying on the same level vertically rather

than suddenly crouching or stretching upward. For instance, if a player is waiting to receive a volleyball serve in a typical squatting position and has to move to get to the ball, it is best for balance if he maintains the squat and moves sideways using a side shuffle or cross-over step. This is because bending the knees lowers the body's center of gravity, and something with a low center of gravity is not likely to topple over.

Staying on the same level also improves quickness, since the individual does not waste time rising up when he realizes he has to move to contact the ball. Coaches often use a quickness drill called a dot drill to help athletes learn this principle. In dot drills the coach places colored dots on the floor in a rectangular pattern. Each player starts with each foot on dots that are across from each other and has to scoot as quickly as possible to land on other dots in a specified pattern.

Members of Cuba's men's volleyball team do stretching exercises as part of their warm-up for a training session. Stretching helps players increase flexibility and avoid injury.

Strength and Power Training

While all these drills help to improve muscle strength and power, volleyball training programs also include exercises that specifically enhance strength and power because they are

Training the Team

Training for a team sport requires individual training and team training. In 1984, while training the U.S. men's team, head coach Doug Beal realized that all his players were outstanding as individuals, but their talents were not being coordinated as a team. Part of the role of a coach is to figure out how to best unify a team into a cohesive unit, and Beal tried moving players around to best achieve this goal. For example, he put players Karch Kiraly and Aldis Berzins on defense rather than strictly using them on offense, and on many plays he began using four hitters coming up from the back row to the front row to pound away at the opposing team. He also took the players on team-building adventures, such as mountain climbing trips, where they had to depend on each other for survival, to foster their working together as a team. The team-building strategies paid off, as the team went on to win an Olympic gold medal.

so critical for explosive, fast-moving volleyball skills. Strength training increases the force an athlete is capable of applying, while power training strives to decrease the time during which the muscle force is applied so maximum force can be maintained without the athlete tiring. While strength training may just involve lifting weights, power training requires the athlete to quickly manipulate light-to-medium weight objects many times. A 2003 study reported in the *Journal of Strength and Conditioning Research* finds that power "is primarily a function of the rate of increase in muscle activation by the nervous system."[25] This means that power-training exercises work to condition the muscles to respond more quickly to signals from the brain and spinal cord. This occurs mostly because these exercises stimulate FT muscle fibers.

The main types of power-training exercises are ballistics and plyometrics. Ballistics involves applying large amounts of force to throwing a medium-weight object, such as a large medicine ball, with both arms, back and forth to another player, using the chest, shoulder, and arm muscles. The fast, repeated motions increase muscle power over time.

In plyometrics an athlete stretches a muscle group just before contracting it to make it contract faster and more forcefully, thus increasing its power. This stretching motion is known as an eccentric action. One commonly employed plyometric exercise uses the eccentric action of squatting before executing a vertical jump. The squat stretches the leg and hip muscles and essentially spring-loads them to store energy. Then, when the athlete extends his legs and jumps up, the stored energy makes the player jump higher than he would have without the squat. The second phase of the movement (the jump) is called a concentric action. Research shows that the faster a concentric action follows an eccentric action, the more powerful the muscles become.

Skill Drills

In addition to the drills that enhance power and other desired qualities, volleyball practice sessions include skill drills to practice specific skills, such as serving, digging, and spiking.

Players on Creighton University's women's volleyball team work on a drill at the net during practice. A team's training session may include several types of drills as well as real-game practice.

Many practices are designed so that each player moves to a different station in a gym to practice each skill and receive feedback from a coach or trainer. This allows each player to work on coordinating their muscle movements and controlling the forces needed for each skill.

As important as these drills are, experts say it is equally important for players to practice playing real games against their teammates during training sessions to coordinate their actions as a team. Practicing the many situations likely to occur during a game not only enhances teamwork, but also strengthens decision making and other psychological factors that are as important as physical and technical performance in determining individual and team success.

CHAPTER 4

Psychology and Volleyball

Volleyball players rely as much on mental qualities, such as thinking, focus, motivation, and emotional resilience, as they do on physical skills to play well. Cecile Reynaud, author of *Coaching Volleyball Technical and Tactical Skills*, writes,

> Volleyball is a quick-moving game that requires players to play hard but smart; maintain focus on their technique while implementing a game plan according to their opponents' strengths and weaknesses; stay positive with their teammates when opponents have the momentum; and stay focused on the next play instead of thinking about what just happened. Most important to volleyball players' success, however, is the mental ability to understand the game and read cues that allow them to execute the proper skill at the right time.[26]

All in the Mind

Sports psychology is a field of psychology that studies and helps all types of athletes develop optimal mental and emotional skills that allow them to consistently perform at their best. Sports psychology is based on the work of Indiana University psychologist Norman Triplett, who published

Kerri Walsh, left, and Misty May-Treanor celebrate their victory in the women's beach volleyball final at the 2012 Olympic Games. The pair consulted a sports psychologist in 2009 to put their game back on track when their level of play inexplicably slumped.

the first studies on social and mental factors in sports in 1898. Triplett demonstrated that the presence of a competitor enhanced athletes' performance in bicycle races, leading mental health experts to realize that the mind, or psyche, plays a huge role in athletic performance. The field of sports psychology developed after the first sports psychology laboratory was founded in Germany in 1920.

Sports psychologists use a variety of talking and behavior therapy methods to help athletes develop positive mental qualities, such as the ability to concentrate and persevere, to give them a competitive edge. Volleyball coaches and trainers also incorporate similar principles into training programs, as studies prove that the best players are both physically and mentally strong. Beach and indoor champion Sinjin Smith says, "All the best athletes don't always win. It's the guys who are able to concentrate and keep their heads in the game."[27]

Some of the best-known players who have benefited from sports psychology are beach volleyball Olympic gold medalists

Misty May-Treanor and Kerri Walsh. In 2009 the duo became uncharacteristically timid and ineffective on the court and sought counseling with sports psychologist Michael Gervais when they could not figure out why. "We were trying to find this easy answer—if we jump higher or move faster—and it was never physical. It was only mental and emotional. … What it came down to was we were afraid of disappointing each other. … Once we realized that it was like 'We've been so silly,'"[28] Walsh explains. The team discovered that one issue contributing to their "funk" was that May-Treanor intended to retire from professional volleyball after the 2012 Olympics to focus on being a wife and mother. Both women were emotional about the upcoming end of their eleven-year partnership, and once they understood this, they were able to talk about it and improve their performance.

Focus and Concentration

For May-Treanor and Walsh, dealing with the mental distractions that upset their concentration was key to resolving their performance problems. Indeed, the ability to concentrate is critical in determining how well any athlete performs, and a variety of factors can disrupt this concentration. One common challenge in volleyball is to stay focused even when an opposing player is deliberately distracting. Many game strategies are designed to wear down and disrupt an opponents' mental calmness. For instance, serving the ball to an opponent who just made a mistake is a common strategy because the individual is already emotionally upset and may not have recovered enough to fully concentrate on receiving the next serve. Or, if a server is consistently serving to one player, an opposing coach may instruct his team to change positions to force the server to either serve to a different person or to target the same player in a new position. Either adjustment creates a distraction, and any distraction increases the chances of a botched play.

A player curls his fingers to gently tap the ball over the net in a move known in volleyball as a dink.

Faking out opponents is another method of toying with their concentration by catching them off guard. In one move called a dink, for example, a hitter pretends she is going to deliver a powerful spike. She forcefully swings her arm, jumps up, and perhaps even grunts with exertion, but at the last second she merely taps the ball to a spot where no defensive players are waiting. Another fake-out is called a cross play. Here, a setter pretends to set the ball up for a hitter

A Fake-out Artist

Sports psychology involves concentration, motivation, attitude, and the importance of mentally overpowering ones' opponents. One method of overpowering an opponent is faking them out. In the 1960s Jungo Morita of the Japanese National Team excelled in faking out his opponents and is credited with innovating two fake-out moves, the pump attack and the snatch spike.

In the pump attack, an offensive hitter makes a short vertical jump to get an opposing blocker to react by jumping up to block a spike. The hitter lands and quickly jumps up again, this time high up, and spikes the ball before the defenders have time to react again.

The snatch spike involves one player passing the ball to a setter, who jumps to supposedly set the ball for a hitter. However, another hitter "snatches" the ball away from the setter by running up and spiking it into the opponents' court without it being set.

who jumps up, but does not hit the ball. Then, another hitter jumps up and fakes a hit, and finally, the real hitter sneaks up and delivers the real hit. Professional beach volleyball player Rob Heidger says, "A good cross play will make your opponents think they are staring at a popcorn machine. Lots of players pop up and down and the true hitter surprises them at the last second."[29]

Other times volleyball players try to derail their opponents' concentration by intimidating them in different ways. Some resort to yelling insults, even though this is against the rules. For example, player Kathy Gregory, who is now the head women's volleyball coach at University of California, Santa Barbara, was known in the 1970s and 1980s for screaming at opponents to distract them.

Others do not use verbal assaults but merely play aggressively to intimidate opponents and break their focus. During the 2012 Olympics, for instance, Walsh and May-Treanor made it clear to their opponents that they were in charge. Walsh said at the time, "We want to attack these teams because they're going to attack us. We're bigger and we're fiercer and we want to impose ourselves on them because if you give them an inch, they'll take a mile."[30]

A player from
South Korea closes
her eyes to sustain
her focus while
her opponents
on the Serbian
team celebrate a
point. The ability
to maintain
concentration
and focus despite
distractions on the
court are critical to
a player's success.

Combating Distractions

With all the distractions that can erupt, good players train themselves not to let intimidation or other tactics interfere with their concentration. Some players achieve this goal better than others. One champion known as much for his superb focus as for his physical skills is Karch Kiraly, winner of Olympic beach and indoor volleyball gold medals in the 1980s and assistant coach of the 2012 USA women's Olympic team. According to the Volleyball Hall of Fame, "Kiraly is known for his overall volleyball skills and his laser-like concentration. He plays volleyball with a hard-driven intensity. His competition is fierce but not mean, his ability to shut the world out, legendary."[31]

Kiraly gained much of his ability to concentrate under pressure after an unpleasant incident at a Los Angeles–area

beach game in 1977. He was playing against Mike Normand, a tough, ex-army special forces soldier, when Normand became angry at something the then-sixteen-year-old Kiraly said and viciously screamed at and threatened Kiraly. Kiraly and the crowd watching the match were frightened to the point of trembling, and Kiraly lost the game. However, Kiraly vowed to never again let anyone intimidate him. He says, "I had never been intimidated before. Not knowing his past … later I found out what Normand could have done to me! … After that match with Normand I could handle any kind of intimidation."[32]

While athletes such as Kiraly may learn some of their focusing and mental toughness skills from unpleasant experiences, more often well-designed coaching programs play a role in fostering these attributes. Good coaches often incorporate focusing exercises into skill drills. For example, in teaching a player to respond to a spiked ball, a coach may initially instruct the player to focus on the arm position of the hitter to anticipate where and how hard the ball will land. Later on, the coach may add in other focus points, such as cueing in on the ball height above the net, to further improve the player's defensive skills and to enhance his ability to focus only on selected things.

The ability to concentrate is especially important during a game, when noise from spectators, referee calls, and other distractions abound. The best athletes learn to tune out these distractions, and focusing exercises during training are invaluable in achieving that goal. Practicing playing real games during training is also helpful, as this helps players learn to rapidly shift their focus as events unfold.

Motivation and Self-Control

Effective coaching can also enhance other important mental skills, such as motivation and self-control. Much of the motivation to learn, practice, and excel comes from within an individual. For example, for some athletes, a desire to qualify for the Olympics is motivation enough to keep working hard. But motivation also comes from coaches and teammates. A coach who has a positive attitude while still challenging

players to improve through rigorous training is much more likely to motivate players than one who is verbally abusive or who ignores players' physical and emotional needs. Coaches who encourage team-building rituals, such as high fives and team chants, are also more likely to motivate players to put forth extra effort for the team.

One volleyball coach known for his motivational skills was Al Scates at the University of California, Los Angeles, who both challenged and encouraged his players. When Scates retired in 2012, Kiraly, who played for Scates, said he "presented a demeanor that was infectious to his athletes."[33] Scates led by example and gave his players the confidence to do their best.

Teammates can also be a source of motivation, and Kiraly himself is widely known for his ability to motivate other players. According to the Volleyball Hall of Fame, "he was the sparkplug that drove the 1984 and 1988 [Olympic] teams because his total dedication to playing superb volleyball encouraged the other players to always play their best."[34]

Another way in which coaches and teammates often motivate others is by encouraging them to maintain control of their emotions and temper. According to an article on the Teen Champion Mindset website, "any loss of control can disrupt not only your performance, but your entire team's as well."[35] Many events, including questionable referee calls and verbal abuse from opponents, can trigger emotional outbursts or poor sportsmanship that can result in penalties and a loss of individual and team concentration.

Sports psychologists recommend many methods of maintaining self-control. Some players, like Kiraly, teach themselves to simply ignore any distractions. Others learn

Beach Volleyball Attire

Beach volleyball attire for women is a controversial issue that has led to strong spectator and player opinions and to controversial rule changes. Some players and women's organizations said that bikinis, which the Fédération Internationale de Volleyball (FIVB) declared to be the official uniform for women's Olympic and other competitive beach volleyball in 1994, detracted from athleticism and were psychologically damaging. Others believed there was nothing wrong with the uniform. In 2007 a temporary change to the uniform was made at the South Pacific Games in Samoa, where religious conservatives' protested that bikinis were immodest. Female players wore shorts and crop tops instead. By 2012, FIVB and Olympic rules were permanently changed to allow women to choose to wear either bikinis or shorts or leggings and sleeved tops.

The divergent opinions about bikinis are exemplified by Australian player Natalie Cook, who believes wearing bikinis in beach volleyball is fine if women wish to wear them, and by International League for Women's Rights spokeswoman Annie Sugier, who disagrees. Cook says, "I believe it [bikini] shows the best side of the female body and I'm proud of how we look in it," while Sugier says, "They are using women's bodies as sex. ... It makes women look like objects and it is a clear case of sexism."

Quoted in Estelle Shirbon. "Olympics—Beach Volleyball—Women Wear Bikinis with Pride." Reuters, July 29, 2012. www.reuters.com/article/2012/07/29/oly-voll-bvvol-day2-bikinis-idUSL6E8IRM7E20120729.

to breathe deeply and count to ten before reacting. By then, they have convinced themselves that a tantrum will not accomplish anything worthwhile. Many coaches constantly reiterate the notion that poor sportsmanship or reacting aggressively to referee calls will double any damage by possibly adding a penalty to the situation.

One player who was once known for not controlling his temper was Tony Ciarelli. His anger over referees' decisions or teammates' mistakes often led him to verbally assault those around him. However, in his senior year at the University of Southern California (USC), Ciarelli realized he could benefit from channeling his emotions into aggressive, skillful playing rather than into unsportsmanlike conduct. For instance, in an April 2012 game against the Cal State Northridge Matadors, the Matadors made the mistake of verbally taunting Ciarelli when they were leading 7–4. As the *Daily Trojan*, the USC campus newspaper, reports, "The [Matadors] took this lead as an opportunity to taunt Ciarelli about the Trojans' loss in the Final Four last season. Bad idea. Ciarelli followed this with two consecutive kills followed by two consecutive blocks to put the Trojans back up."[36]

Motor Learning

As important as emotional control, motivation, and concentration are in volleyball performance, an equally critical mental element emphasized in training programs is motor learning. This involves training the nervous system and muscles to automatically work in harmony to execute certain skills. In his book, *The Science of Volleyball Practice Development and Drill Design*, Edward Spooner explains that reacting automatically to conditions in a game is essential in a fast-moving game because

a volleyball player who digs a ball hit at over 60 miles per hour must anticipate the speed of the ball, the reaction time available in relation to the incoming ball and the point of contact while executing the required motor program. This action takes place so quickly (less than a second) that conscious thought is virtually impossible and skill execution at this point in performance has now become virtually automatic.[37]

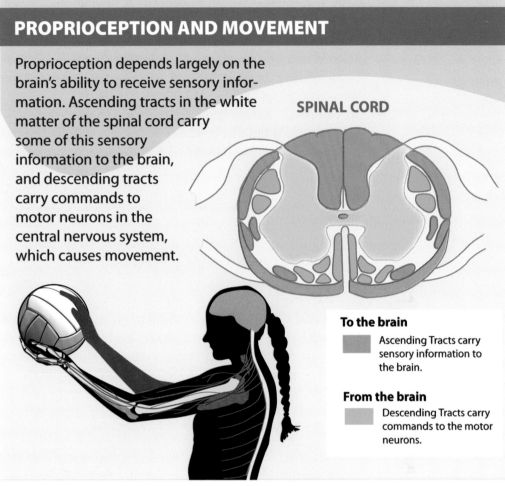

PROPRIOCEPTION AND MOVEMENT

Proprioception depends largely on the brain's ability to receive sensory information. Ascending tracts in the white matter of the spinal cord carry some of this sensory information to the brain, and descending tracts carry commands to motor neurons in the central nervous system, which causes movement.

SPINAL CORD

To the brain
Ascending Tracts carry sensory information to the brain.

From the brain
Descending Tracts carry commands to the motor neurons.

Adapted from http://blog.aglamslam.com/wp-content/uploads/2012/04/Picture-3.png, http://classconnection.s3.amazonaws.com/1527/flashcards/688632/png/lskdjf.png

Motor learning relies on the scientific principles of proprioception and kinesthetic awareness. Proprioception is the ability of the brain and spinal cord to coordinate the body so it stays upright, and kinesthetic awareness is an individual's ability to judge where his body is in relation to his surroundings. Both influence individual and team performance, and both can be improved with practice. For example, by practicing a forearm pass many times, a volleyball player learns exactly how her arms must be placed on the ball, how much her legs must bend to keep her balance, and how much force she must apply to get the ball accurately to a teammate.

Through practice, her proprioception and kinesthetic awareness abilities become automatic, so she can execute a skill without thinking about each step.

Part of proprioception and kinesthetic awareness comes from coordinating incoming sensory information with movement. Eye-body coordination is especially important in volleyball. When the eyes see a ball being served, for example, with practice a player learns to mentally measure the speed and angle of the ball's approach and automatically

Energy-Saving Motor Learning

Recent studies show that motor learning not only enhances athletic performance, but also saves energy. Once athletic skills become part of an individual's memory bank of automatic motions, he is able to perform the skills longer and faster without becoming as tired as occurred earlier in the learning process. This is because motor learning trains an athlete's body to execute skills in the most energy-efficient way.

One study that supports this finding was performed in 2005 at the University of Tsukuba in Japan. It revealed that inexperienced volleyball players start moving the shoulder of their hitting arm toward the middle of their body earlier during a spike hit than elite players do. Inexperienced players also extend the elbow of the hitting arm for a longer period of time than elite athletes do. The increased shoulder movement and elbow extension result in much greater angular velocity in the elbow and more stress on the shoulder joint, leading to greater fatigue. Since peak muscle power occurs at 40 to 60 percent of maximum angular velocity, inexperienced players also generate a less powerful spike. Through motor learning, elite athletes train their bodies to conserve energy while still generating powerful hits, exemplifying the complex interactions between mental and physical factors in athletic performance.

instructs the rest of the body to respond by moving toward the ball and connecting with the hands or arms. The brain moderates motor learning by comparing new incoming sensory information with stored memories of similar situations, then recruiting the right muscles to respond based on this comparison. The more experience and practice a player has, the more stored motor skills programs he can draw on without taking the time to figure out what to do.

Feedback and Visualization

Another important element in motor learning is internal and external feedback. External feedback comes from the coaches who help athletes learn skills by making them aware of what is needed for improvement. For instance, a coach might tell and demonstrate to a player that his passing skills will improve if he extends his arms at a forty-five degree angle. The player can then incorporate this feedback into internal feedback, which involves his muscles, joints, and other body parts letting his brain know how they are positioned when successfully executing a particular skill. Once the brain coordinates this feedback, the athlete becomes increasingly adept at performing the skill without having to stop to think about it.

Sports psychologists often recommend a technique called visualization to help athletes enhance the effects of feedback on motor learning. Visualization simply involves imagining how something looks or feels before doing it. One study shows that volleyball players who visualize how completing a perfect pass looks before participating in passing drills perform better than other players. Other studies indicate that beginners who visualize themselves correctly performing skills learn the skills faster than those who do not.

In addition to visualization, another technique coaches and sports psychologists recommend for enhancing motor learning is breaking a complex skill into small steps. Rather than demonstrating or teaching a complete serve, a coach might first focus a player's attention on practicing the approach to the baseline. When this skill is mastered, he may then focus on teaching the person to

A player on Brazil's women's volleyball team practices under the watchful eye of her coach, who will provide her and her teammates with feedback they can use to refine their skill and technique.

perfect the ball toss, followed by the arm swing. Mastering each small step allows the brain to coordinate and merge the correct steps together into a complete action without being distracted by repeatedly discarding elements that were performed incorrectly.

Breaking down goals into small steps not only helps the brain organize motor skills, but also prevents athletes from becoming overwhelmed by a failure to properly execute a complete skill right away. Focusing on small steps can also keep advanced players on track by not allowing them to become overwhelmed by long-term goals or career plans. A teenager once asked Kiraly how he prepared to win his

Olympic medals, and Kiraly replied, "I never did. I only prepared to win the next play."[38]

Mental Muscle

Motor learning improves a player's overall tactical intelligence because he can focus on playing smart rather than spending time on analyzing every movement. When the entire team plays smart, it enhances team spirit and motivation, which can play a huge role in pushing everyone to try harder to achieve success. The role of both mental and physical power in determining athletic performance is complex and intertwined, but experts agree that both elements are essential.

CHAPTER 5

The Biomechanics of Offense

Volleyball players and teams need to practice and perfect the mental and physical skills needed to succeed in order to work in technical and tactical harmony, whether on offense or defense. The primary offensive, or attacking, skills are serving, setting, and hitting. These movements all depend on the biomechanical skills of coordination, balance, agility, flexibility, strength, and power and on the mental development of motor learning that takes place during training and conditioning.

Setting Up the Offense

The basic goals of offensive plays are to either complete a service ace (a serve that cannot be returned) or to set up the ball so a hitter can spike or tap it over the net and have it land on the ground (a kill). According to K. Lee Lerner and Brenda Wilmoth Lerner in their book, *World of Sports Science*, "the set and spike mechanism is the most effective offensive series that can be executed in volleyball."[39]

Although tall, powerful hitters receive much of the glory in volleyball, being a good setter (someone who sets up the ball for a kill) is athletically just as challenging because it relies on control and finesse. Being tall is not advantageous for a setter, but a setter must be agile, quick, flexible, and

A setter gets his body into the ready position as a serve comes his way in order to make effective contact with the ball. He will use both his arms and legs to exert force on the ball during his set.

strong, and must coordinate perfect timing with the ability to apply the right amount of force to put the ball where the hitter needs it. This takes a great deal of practice. In discussing the importance of a good setter, an article on the website Volleyball Training Ground.com states, "The setter is to volleyball what the quarterback is to football. They are running the show and calling out the plays and running the offense for the team. It is their job to make sure the ball is where it needs to be so that a hitter can put it away."[40]

A setter can set (place the ball in the air for a hitter) in front or in back of herself, usually with her feet planted on the ground. Sometimes, though, a setter performs a jump set where he jumps up to set the ball quickly, before the opposing team can launch a defense. The jump set requires even more practice than other sets because it is easier to accidentally hit the ball illegally with the palms of the hands while jumping.

Any type of set starts with a ready position and relies on muscles throughout the body. In the ready stance, the player's feet are shoulder-width apart with one foot slightly forward

A Powerful Hitter

Outside hitter Flo Hyman was known for both her athletic prowess and positive attitude. Born in Los Angeles, California, on July 31, 1954, the 6-foot-5-inch Hyman was initially self-conscious about her height as a teenager but soon realized it could help her excel in sports. She played basketball and ran track in high school but only dabbled in recreational beach volleyball until she was recruited by a volleyball coach at the University of Houston and received the school's first female athletic scholarship.

Another first for Hyman was that she was one of the first African Americans to play competitive volleyball. She excelled to the point of being a three-time collegiate All-American and receiving the U.S. Volleyball Association's Most Valuable Player award in 1977. She earned a spot on the 1980 and 1984 U.S. women's Olympic teams but, like the other 1980 Olympians, did not participate that year because of the U.S. boycott of the Moscow Olympics. As team captain in 1984, Hyman played a huge role, both athletically and motivationally, in leading her team to win a silver medal.

Hyman then became a professional volleyball player but tragically collapsed and died during a game in Japan on January 24, 1986. An autopsy revealed that, unbeknownst to her, she had Marfan syndrome, a connective tissue disease that affected her heart.

and both knees bent to improve balance and stability. The upper body leans slightly forward. The player observes where the ball will come down and moves to contact it, with his shoulders and hips facing the direction where he wants the ball to go. He then extends his arms overhead, with the fingers spread to form a triangle in front of his forehead. When the ball arrives, he makes contact with the fingertips of both hands, with the arms and knees still bent. The ball cannot touch the palms or a referee will call an illegal touch. The legs, arms, and wrists then extend to push the ball upward and forward, and the arms follow through by remaining overhead for a few seconds to help with balance.

A study by kinesiologists at Texas Women's University found that the most active joints during a set are the shoulder, elbow, and knee, and the main way in which setters control the force they exert on the ball is by controlling the amount they extend the arms and legs to push the ball upward and forward. Accurate setters learn that the farther away from the hitter they are, the more they must extend the arms and legs to transfer additional momentum to the ball so it travels farther.

Effective Hitting

Sheer power is more important for hitters than for setters, but coordination, quickness, and agility also play an important role in hitting. Whether the hitter hits the ball from the front or back row, a quick, carefully coordinated attack is critical. Most hits are launched from the front row, right at the net.

The hitter starts in a ready position with the shoulders and trunk angled slightly forward of the feet, with the arms loose at the sides. The right foot should be a bit in front of the left in a right-handed player. When the ball arrives at its highest point after being positioned by the setter, the hitter begins a two-, three-, or four-step approach. The number of steps depends on how far away the ball is. In a

A hitter jumps as she prepares to make contact with a ball that has been set for her. Timing and balance are key to an effective hit.

four-step approach, the first step moves the hitter closer to the ball, with the arms still relaxed. In the second step he swings his arms straight out behind his back and steps into what is known as a foot plant. Here, the left foot goes slightly in front of the right foot, with the knees slightly bent and the feet and hips at a forty-five degree angle to the net. The next one or two steps launch the vertical jump that is critical to the success of a hit, and volleyball coaches say the speed and timing of the entire approach is important in determining the quality of the jump. "A strong approach is critical for attaining maximum jump and making contact with the ball at its highest point,"[41] write coaches Bonnie Kenny and Cindy Gregory in their book, *Volleyball: Steps to Success*.

The first two steps in the approach are short and slow; the last two are bigger and faster. The key is making the last two steps as quick as possible while maintaining balance. The Strength and Power for Volleyball.com website explains, "The shorter the ground contact time is on the last two steps of the approach the more elastic energy [momentum] you can utilize for exploding high."[42]

Exploding Into a Jump

During the step leading into the jump, the hitter swings both arms from behind his body and lifts his arms upward. The arm swings increase the power of the jump by about 15 percent, making it go higher and faster due to the muscle energy from the arms adding momentum and increasing the ground reaction force that pushes the body upward. The strength and flexibility of the legs also play a big role in the speed and height of the jump. The quadriceps muscles in the front of the thighs produce much of the power for the jump, and studies show that this power is greatest in athletes with flexible hamstring muscles in back of the thighs. This is because tight hamstrings hold back the quadriceps and prevent them from exerting maximum power. The hamstrings and quadriceps are what is known as opposing muscle groups. That is, they do opposite things. When tightness prevents the hamstrings from properly doing their job, the quadriceps must work extra hard to balance the muscle forces in the legs, and they lose some of their power.

Studies also show that muscles in the hips and ankles are important in providing jumping power during a hit, while

A hitter uses the swing of his arms and the strength and flexibility of his legs to achieve a high vertical leap. By making contact with the ball at his maximum height, he increases the power of his strike.

those in the knees are more active in absorbing forces during the landing from the jump. "Knee muscles contribute significantly to the performance of a vertical jump, however the muscle groups surrounding the hip and ankle were found to generate the most energy . . . muscles crossing the hip and ankle produce energy while muscles crossing the knee absorbed energy,"[43] according to a study conducted at San Jose State University.

As the hitter jumps, he ideally hits the ball at the high point of the jump. This is because, as a Taiwanese study reports, "the higher the spiking point, the higher the spiking height, the harder for the opponent to block the ball."[44] Hitters thus strive to achieve the highest possible jump and ball strike point, since both affect the power of the hit. Many elite volleyball players can achieve a vertical jump height of 40 or more inches (102cm). The highest-known vertical jump height for a volleyball player is 50 inches (127cm), performed by Leonel Marshall of the Cuban Men's National Team. Vertical jump velocities of as much as 14 feet (4.3m) per second and striking points of about 10 feet (3m) high have been reported for high-jumping athletes.

In executing the spike, the hitter pulls her hitting arm and shoulder back and holds the elbow and hand as high as possible. As the hitting arm and hand swing forward to contact the ball with an open hand, the opposite arm pulls down to the chest. The place on the ball that the hand strikes determines the angle at which the ball arrives in the opponents' court, and the speed and power of the ball are determined by the rotation of the wrist, hips, and shoulders as well as by the height and velocity of the jump. Rotating and snapping the wrist to add topspin as the hand strikes the ball adds speed to the ball because of the Magnus effect, and rotating the hips and shoulders at the peak of the jump adds speed and power by increasing the amount of angular momentum being transferred to the ball.

Learning to coordinate a jump while simultaneously adding topspin and rotating the body takes a great deal of practice, especially since the athlete is also simultaneously assessing the opposing blockers' positions to best place the ball, and trying to avoid touching the net and gaining a penalty. The best hitters learn to incorporate all these elements of skill and tactical intelligence to deliver crushing, powerful hits. Elite male hitters are known to hit spikes at up to 60 miles per hour (97kmh) and females up to 38 miles per hour (61kmh).

One beach/indoor champion known for his powerful spikes was Gene Selznick, who pioneered competitive beach volleyball in Southern California in the 1950s and 1960s. His hits were so forceful that a 1969 *Los Angeles Times* article half-jokingly stated, "There are still State Beach hangers-on who are convinced that the recent oil seepage off Santa Barbara resulted from reverberations from Selznick cannon shots pounded into the sand."[45]

Spikes and Serves

The physics and biomechanics of spike hits are similar to those involved in the other main offensive move, the serve, although there are some differences which depend on the type of serve. The main differences between serves and spike hits are that a serve travels farther than a spike hit and that a hitter receives the ball from a setter during a spike, but during a serve, a server puts the ball in play by tossing it up. This means that a serve is executed slower than a spike hit because the server does not have to rush to intercept a ball put in play by someone else. While a server cannot wait indefinitely to launch the serve after he stands behind the baseline, he does have more time to think about which type of serve to deliver for maximum tactical advantage. As Cecile Reynaud

THE UNDERHAND SERVE

In an underhand serve, the player begins by swinging her serving arm back, using her muscles to create potential energy at the top of the swing. When the player brings her arm down, she is transferring the downward momentum of her swing to the ball, which combines with the power exerted by her muscles to make the ball airborne and send it over the net.

writes in his book, *Coaching Volleyball Technical and Tactical Skills*, "serving is the only skill in volleyball where the individual player is in complete control of the ball."[46]

There are several types of serves, including underhand, sidearm, roundhouse, jump, float, and various combinations. The most commonly used serves in competitive volleyball are float and jump serves. Good servers master several types of serves to keep their opponents guessing about which one they will use, but this decision is also influenced by the amount of control the server has over each type of serve. Powerful jump serves are the most difficult to control, and each player must weigh the advantages of accurately placing a simpler serve within the court boundaries against the advantages of completing the most powerful serve in the game.

The Float Serve

In a float serve the server stands behind the baseline with the foot corresponding to the nonhitting arm slightly forward, with both knees bent. The nonhitting hand holds the ball with the arm outstretched at shoulder level in front of the hitting arm's shoulder. As the server tosses the ball up, ideally 12 to 18 inches (30 to 46 cm) above the shoulder, she brings her hitting arm back with the elbow bent and the hand close to the ear. Both shoulders rotate back toward the hitting arm, and the server watches the ball so she can hit it as it reaches its highest point, while twisting the hip, shoulder, elbow, wrist, and hand and contacting the ball below its center with an open hand or half-closed fist. As the hand hits the ball, the server may transfer her weight to her front foot or take a small step to add forward momentum and power to the serve.

Float serves do not include spin, but the ball follows an erratic, wobbling flight path due to the boundary layer asymmetry caused by indentations on the ball. Opponents therefore have trouble determining where the ball will land.

Executing a float serve relies on muscles throughout the body, but the forces put out by these muscles are less than those involved in spike hits or jump serves. The legs and feet

A server puts her body into proper motion in order to deliver a float serve, which will involve a rotation of her torso and a shifting of her body weight to properly complete.

barely move during a float serve, and muscle activity in the teres major, subscapularis, pectoralis major, and latissimus dorsi muscles in the shoulder of the hitting arm is far less than that seen in these other skills.

Basketball and Volleyball

Because height and jumping ability are important for some volleyball positions, quite a few volleyball players are former or current basketball players. Kirk Kilgour was one volleyball player who started off as a basketball player and switched to playing volleyball at the University of California, Los Angeles in the 1960s. Keith Erickson of the 1964 U.S. men's Olympic team did the opposite; switching to professional basketball after playing Olympic volleyball.

The most famous professional basketball star who went on to play professional volleyball was the 7-foot-1-inch-tall Wilt Chamberlain. After a stellar career in the National Basketball Association (NBA), Chamberlain took up beach volleyball while recovering from knee surgery. He went on to start and play on a professional volleyball team called Wilt's Big Dippers and helped start the International Volleyball Association (IVA) in 1976. Despite Chamberlain's efforts to keep the IVA alive, it folded by 1979.

The Jump Serve

Rather than relying on an erratic flight path, a jump serve seeks to maximize the ball's speed to prevent opponents from being able to return it. Although it is the most difficult serve to control, the jump serve is the fastest, most powerful serve out there. Elite mens' jump serves are known to travel up to 44 miles per hour (71kmh) and females' up to 29 miles per hour (476kmh). As in a spike hit, the speed and power come from the jump, body rotation, and topspin put on the ball.

A server starts a jump serve about 16 feet, 4 inches (5m) behind the court baseline, then runs up to the line, tosses the ball, jumps, and hits the ball in a manner similar to that in a spike hit. In an article on the Coachesinfo.com website, biomechanics experts Marion Alexander and Adrian Honish write, "The spike serve has many similarities to the spike itself. The player strikes the ball with maximum force at the peak of his jump, and tries to place it so that the opposing player cannot receive it cleanly."[47]

The higher the ball toss and the jump, the higher the point of impact with the ball and the greater the ball's speed will be. Putting topspin on the ball also increases the speed. Studies show that adding topspin to a jump serve can reduce the ball's time in the air by about one-tenth of a second. While this seems like a small amount, it can make a big difference in an opponent's ability to respond to the serve. The speed of the topspin determines how much faster the ball drops, and a faster spin results from a faster and more extensive wrist snap. The faster the spin, the faster the ball drops.

A player leaps to deliver a jump serve, which uses power and speed to increase the opponent's difficulty in returning the ball. The serves of elite male players have been known to travel up to 44 miles per hour (72 km/hr).

Science Fiction–Like Jumps

One of the women's volleyball standouts in the 2012 Olympics was the 6-foot-4-inch-tall Destinee Hooker, who is known for her almost supernatural jumping and spiking ability. According to Juliet Macur, writing in the New York Times, "when she leaps, she rises from the ground so high and with such ease that she looks suspended midair, like a character from The Matrix. At her best, she can reach 11 feet 2 inches—or 1 foot 2 inches higher than a basketball rim. And when she hits the ball at the height of her leap, most of the time there is no stopping her."

Some of Hooker's jumping and athletic ability comes from her genes. Her father, Ricky, played basketball for the San Antonio Spurs and sister, Marshevet, excelled in track and field and was on the 2008 U.S. Olympic team. The other part of Hooker's success comes from hard work and a constant striving to improve. In high school she excelled in basketball, volleyball, and track and field, and in college she earned honors as a track and field high jumper as well as in volleyball. In 2011 she was named best spiker in the Fédération Internationale de Volleyball World Cup competition and received the same honor in the 2012 Olympics.

Juliet Macur. "A Force from Above as U.S. Reaches Final." *New York Times*, August 9, 2012. www.nytimes.com/2012/08/10/ sports/olympics/destinee-hooker-leads-olympic-volleyball-team-to-gold-medal-match.html?_r=0.

Coordinating and perfectly timing the run up, toss, jump, and hit with topspin is challenging and takes much practice. In fact, Alexander and Honish point out that mastering each of these individual skills, particularly the ball toss, is very challenging in itself. They write, "An accurate toss is an important aspect of the skilled spike serve, and takes many years of practice to perfect the exact timing, direction, and height required for a reliable serve."[48]

Biomechanics of a Jump Serve

Because of the toss, the biomechanics of the jump serve are somewhat different than those in a spike hit. In most overhand serves, the server tosses the ball with his nonhitting arm. However, studies show that tossing the ball with the hitting arm in a jump serve results in greater momentum being transferred to the ball when the ball is hit and in greater lift forces for the jump. After the ball is tossed, both the hitting and nonhitting arms go

downward, then extend upward to help power the jump. This is especially effective when coordinated with the extension of the bent knees, which also lift the jump. "Skilled servers perform the upward swing of the arms while the flexed knees are starting to extend so that the arm swing can contribute to the ground reaction forces acting upward on the server,"[49] explain Alexander and Honish. As the arms swing upward, they push down on nearby joints, and this increases the downward forces on the floor. In turn this increases the ground reaction force acting on the athlete, per Newton's third law.

While jumping, the server begins to swing her hitting arm back from the vertical and rotates her shoulder so it is sideways to the net. When one body part rotates in one direction, according to the laws of physics that govern angular motion (rotation) of an airborne body, another body part must move in the opposite direction to balance the forces acting on the joints. The hips thus rotate backward, and the combined forces from the shoulder and hip rotations add even more power to the jump serve.

The type of force that acts on a rotating object is called torque. Torque refers to both the amount and direction of the force. The sum of the torques generated by the server's rotating body, plus the ground reaction force, momentum from the arm swing, and speed at which the hand strikes the ball, all contribute to the power of the serve. After the ball is hit, the server's arm follows through by moving across his body to slow down the arm and help the individual balance as he lands on both feet.

The ultimate goal of a serve or a hit, no matter its type, is to score an ace or a kill. Conversely, the goal of the team that receives the serve or hit is to launch a successful defense that involves either blocking or digging and passing.

CHAPTER **6**

Digging into Defense

As important as a good offense is for scoring points, a volleyball team's defensive skills in receiving serves and blocking or otherwise responding to hits are equally critical. Without a good defense, offensive plays cannot be set in motion. The main defensive skills in volleyball are digging (scooping or lifting) up and blocking the ball before it hits the ground. Blockers usually stand in the front row and jump up to put the ball back into the opponent's court before it gets over the net. Being tall is advantageous for this skill, and many elite blockers are well over 6 feet tall.

For back-row defensive players, including liberos, height is not critical. Each team is allowed to designate one libero, who wears a contrasting jersey color and who exclusively plays in the back row. His purpose is to be an expert digger and passer, although other team members can dig and pass the ball as well.

In some ways, being a libero is less physically demanding than being a hitter or blocker who jumps and swings their arms repeatedly. However, liberos often perform physically taxing moves where they run and dive to the floor and do repeated low squats, so they must be strong, quick, flexible, and agile.

Clues for Defensive Players

One way defensive volleyball players can enhance their skills is by observing and analyzing their opponents' body movements for clues about where and how fast the ball will arrive. Some of these clues include:

- When a hitter approaches the ball quickly, the hit will likely be fast and hard because the person's momentum transfers to the jump and spike.
- Watching the direction of the hitter's shoulders reveals where the ball will land. The ball goes in the direction the hitter's shoulders are facing.
- A hitter's fast arm swing means a fast-moving ball. A slow arm swing means a gentle tap or slower-moving ball.
- When the hitter's hitting arm elbow drops below his ear, the shot will probably be a tip, or gentle tap.
- If the hitter hits the ball on its underside, the ball will go upward and not be spiked downward.

Can You Dig It?

Liberos and other players who dig out and pass the ball must also have excellent judgment and coordination skills to respond effectively to serves and spikes that can approach at speeds close to that of cars zooming on a freeway. Volleyball teams depend on focused, accurate diggers to not only rescue the ball from touching the ground but also to complete accurate passes that allow offensive plays to be launched. In the book, *Biomechanics in Sports V*, biomechanics experts M.E. Ridgeway and N. Hamilton write, "Every offensive play begins with a pass. . . . Today's quick paced game has created an even greater need for exact, consistent passing."[50]

To prepare for a dig and pass, the player hunches down with knees bent and feet shoulder-width apart, with one foot slightly forward. The head is slightly in front of the legs, and the arms hang in front of the knees with the hands open. This position is similar to the ready position of a shortstop in baseball.

While anticipating the ball, the player must be aware of where his teammates are so he can decide whether to receive the ball or let a teammate do so. He must also focus on the server or hitter across the net to assess the height of the hitter's jump and the speed and direction of the ball. Then he and his teammates communicate this information to each other so everyone knows who will receive the ball.

When the athlete realizes she will receive the ball, she quickly moves to an area right behind its landing spot, maintaining her ready position. She then extends her arms in front of her body and puts the arms together facing upward, with the thumbs close together, to form a flat platform, and gets the platform underneath the ball so she can hit it with the fleshy part of the forearms. This is known as a forearm pass, or bump, and is the most commonly used pass in volleyball.

Coordinating the Pass

Eye-hand coordination is important in connecting the ball with the platform, and the digger must also keep his target teammate in view. In most cases, writes Cecile Reynaud in his book, *Coaching Volleyball Technical and Tactical Skills*, "the intended target for a serve reception (or free ball) is just to the right side of the middle of the court, so the player should angle the platform in that direction and transfer the weight to the right foot in the direction of this target area as contact is made."[51]

Controlling the pass so it reaches its target takes a great deal of practice. Inexperienced players often pass off of the thumbs or wrists, rather than off the fleshy part of the forearms, and this does not allow the player's body to absorb as much of the incoming force of the ball. This makes the ball go higher and faster than it should, so it is more difficult for the setter to receive it and to perform an accurate set. This greater difficulty results from the fact that a higher-up ball accelerates more than a lower-flying ball does as it drops due to gravity, so it is traveling faster when it reaches the setter.

Free-falling objects accelerate at a rate of 32 feet (9.8m) per second per second due to the force of gravity. This number is known in physics as g, or the acceleration of gravity. The higher up an object is, the farther it travels during its descent and the more it speeds up as it travels this distance. For example, one second after a volleyball drops, its velocity is -32 feet (-9.8m) per second. After two seconds, the velocity is -64 feet (-19.6m) per second. By the time it reaches the ground, it is going much faster than a ball that started out lower down would be.

A beach volleyball player positions his body, forearms, and hands in order to make effective contact with the ball. The fleshy part of his forearms can absorb some of the ball's force and better control the height and speed of a pass.

Experienced diggers learn to gain control over the height and speed of a pass by connecting with the ball at the fleshiest part of the forearms and by keeping the arms straight, yet flexible enough to absorb much of the force of the ball's momentum. Absorbing this force ensures that the ball slows down enough that the digger can take control of how high and fast the pass travels.

Other Digging Moves

Depending on the speed and angle of approach of an incoming ball, a digger may use other skills and types of passes in an attempt to get the ball to a teammate. When the ball arrives high up and not too fast, the digger may use an overhead dig and pass. Here, the individual assumes a ready position like that in a forearm dig, then moves underneath the ball when it arrives and straightens her body, extends her arms and hands overhead with the fingers spread apart, and hits the ball upward and forward with the pads of the fingers. In an alternative overhead dig, the digger puts his hands together with the fingers interlocked or the hands wrapped around each other. This position is known as the tomahawk. The ball is hit with the bottom of the hands, and afterward the arms remain up for a few seconds to help with

An Austrian player competing in the 2008 Olympic Games attempts to save a ball from going out of bounds by kicking it over the net—a move which is legal according to the rules of both beach and indoor volleyball.

Nicole Davis

Nicole Davis is an outstanding libero who helped the 2008 and 2012 U.S. women's Olympic teams win silver medals. Born on April 24, 1982, in Stockton, California, the 5-foot-4-inch-tall Davis achieved 705 kills, 1257 digs, 103 aces, and 82 blocks during her high school volleyball years. At the University of Southern California she led her team to a National Collegiate Athletic Association (NCAA) National Championship by averaging 4.25 digs per game and finished her college years with 1,093 total digs. In the 2012 Olympics she started in all eight matches in which her team played and averaged 3.63 digs per game, ranking as the second best libero at the Olympics.

Known as an enthusiastic team player, Davis says, "The most rewarding parts of playing volleyball are the connections you make with your teammates, and the way the game facilitates growth, individually and collectively. I don't remember the spectacular plays after years pass, I remember the moments with my teammates."

Quoted in Team USA. "Nicole Davis USA Volleyball." Team USA. www.teamusa.org/Athletes/DA/Nicole-Davis.aspx.

balance. This follow-through also helps guide the ball in the desired direction.

In situations where a teammate accidentally hits the ball out of bounds on his own side of the court, a defensive player may race to try to save it some distance from the court boundaries to keep it in play. This may call for some creativity in contacting the ball before it hits the ground. Sometimes defensive players manage to get in a hand or arm pass of some sort, but on rare occasions a player will use her feet. This happened in the 2012 Olympics in London, England, when Fabiana Oliveira of the Brazilian women's volleyball team chased down a ball that went past her team's baseline in a game against South Korea. Unable to reach the ball with her hands, Oliveira, who also plays soccer,

SET AND SPIKE

Elite volleyball players can achieve a vertical velocity of about 14 feet (4.3m) per second when they jump up.

jumped up and did a bicycle (scissors) kick, sending the ball backward over her head. Her incredulous teammates received the pass and won the point, and sports commentators labeled the play one of the highlights of the Olympics. Although volleyball players rarely dig and pass with their feet, this move is entirely legal. Prior to 1992, contacting the ball with body parts below the waist was only allowed in beach volleyball. However, a rules change in 1992 now permits this in indoor volleyball as well.

When Player Meets Floor

In other rescue situations, particularly when the ball is arriving fast and low, a defensive player may resort to various diving or collapsing moves that require great flexibility, agility, balance, coordination, muscle strength, and courage in a desperate attempt to keep the ball in play. One coach advises, "The most important thing you'll need to learn to be a great center back is to become absolutely fearless. You'll have to sacrifice your body in a hundred different ways, trying with everything you have to save anything you have the remotest chance of saving. Remember the adage: make the play first, then decide if it was impossible."[52]

One rescue move that involves a trip to the floor is a barrel or log roll, where a player who realizes the ball is about to hit the ground lunges toward the ball, drops his hips, extends the leg closest to the ball, and rolls the body over the bent leg onto the floor. He then performs a forearm pass if possible. If there is no time to put the arms together for the dig and pass, one arm can be used. After the ball is hit, the digger's outside arm slides along the floor to absorb the body's momentum. The extended knee rotates inward so the hips and buttocks gently hit the floor. As the body's momentum slows, the player rolls onto his back with one leg extended and one bent off the floor. Then he rolls onto his stomach, bends the inner leg, and pushes against the floor with both hands to get up.

THE BARREL ROLL

The barrel roll (also known as a shoulder roll or log roll) is one way that a player can make an emergency dig. After saving the ball, the player rolls her body onto the ground. This helps to avoid injury, as the player's body and its momentum make contact with the ground. This roll also allows the player to rise quickly and return to the game.

Adapted from www.theandrewsinstitute.com/InjuryPrevention/Volleyball/, http://peterkaphysics4-5.wikispaces.com/Nicole+Obermaier

Another rescue dig, the sprawl or collapse dig, is used when the ball is about to land right in front of the digger and she has no time to move in any direction except down. The object of a collapse dig is to stretch the arms along the floor and get them under the ball before it hits the ground. The digger raises her heels and crouches as low as possible while lunging with the foot closest to the ball, then stretches out her arms, puts her hands together so the forearms form a platform, and slides the platform under the ball. As she hits the ball upward, she rotates the knee of the lunging leg outward so her body collapses onto her stomach without the knee or hip bones hitting the floor. The low squat and limb rotations require much strength and flexibility to prevent muscle tears and to adequately control which parts of the body hit the ground for the least-painful impact.

These rescue digs do not allow superaccurate, forceful passes because of the awkward positions from which they are executed, but they often do prevent the opponents from scoring a point. This is especially true of the last-resort move called the pancake, which Reynaud describes as "the last option to use when the player can't reach the ball any other way."[53] In the pancake, the digger lowers his hips and lunges toward the ball, extending his body face down on the floor. Balancing on the hands and one knee, he reaches out with one arm and plants that hand flat against the floor with the fingers spread out. The move must be timed so the ball bounces off the back of the hand, and a teammate must be nearby to intercept and pass the ball because this type of hit offers no ball control.

Blocking at the Net

Unlike digging which occurs close to the ground, the other main defensive move, blocking, occurs at the net while jumping to prevent the ball from crossing that net. Many teams have three or more blockers lined up to create a defensive wall that the ball cannot breach.

In preparation for a block, the player stands with his feet shoulder-width apart, knees slightly bent, and heels slightly raised. The elbows are at shoulder height with the forearms held up at a forty-five degree angle to the net and the fingers spread wide. Once the blocker recognizes where the opposing hitter will be, he moves to the side using a side shuffle, crossover step, or running step that puts him opposite the hitter.

The blocker then launches a vertical jump in a manner similar to that used in a spike hit or jump serve, with the arms swinging upward and the knees bending first to increase the height of the jump. According to biomechanics experts Marion Alexander and Adrian Honish, "timing is the key to an effective block and the jump must be timed so that the blocker jumps immediately after the attacker jumps, depending on how far the hitter is from the net. The further

off the net the hitter is hitting the ball, the later the jump."[54] Through experience, blockers learn that it only takes a few fractions of a second more for the ball to travel from a hitter who is a few feet away from the net than it does from one who is right at the net. They use these calculations, plus the knowledge that hitters hit the ball approximately 0.34 seconds after they jump, to decide when to launch their own jump. The blocker must start his jump before the hitter connects with the ball, or it is usually too late to block the hit.

After swinging the arms to help with the jump, the blocker holds the arms still, straight overhead, to increase the height of the jump a bit more. At the high point of the jump, the blocker reaches her hands forward over the net, without touching the net, to deflect the ball downward. The farther over the net she can reach, the more effective the block will be. The blocker's height and the length of her arms, along with the height of the jump, determine how far over the net she can reach. This is why many good blockers are tall.

The biomechanics of a block jump differ somewhat from those of a spike hit or jump serve because the blocker reaches

A row of blockers leap with their arms and hands extended in order to deflect a spike from the opposing team. Muscle strength and timing are keys to effective blocking.

Not an Easy Job

The rules of volleyball are very specific about the ways in which the ball can be touched, passed, hit, or otherwise handled. These rules, plus the fast-moving nature of the game, make it a difficult sport to referee. Since slight differences in referees' opinions about where a player's hand touched the ball or about whether a ball fell in or out of bounds can lead to penalties and perhaps even to lost games, volleyball referees are often not the most popular people around. According to J. Edmund Welch in his book, *How to Play and Teach Volleyball,* "volleyball is probably the most difficult game to referee, since the ball may not come to rest for a period of time. It may not be held, carried, or thrown, as in most other sports. It must be 'clearly hit.' This means there cannot be any follow-through to speak of, or the ball is carried, lifted, or thrown. Therefore, one referee may see a play slightly different from another referee."

J. Edmund Welch. *How to Play and Teach Volleyball.* New York: Association Press, 1960, p. 127.

over the net with both arms. This changes the angles at which the joints flex and stretch. Most notably, the extreme forward shoulder extension causes the hips and trunk to flex backward to balance the torques created by the forward-moving shoulders. This leads to a characteristic jackknife or pike position during the jump. The pike position helps prevent the blocker from committing the error of touching the net and also helps balance his body so he can land straight on both feet. Before landing, however, he must raise his arms straight overhead again so they will not touch the net during his descent.

Blockers, like hitters, may jump and swing their arms twenty or more times per game and much more in practice, and these actions put a great deal of stress on the joints, particularly those in the shoulders and legs. In fact, repetitive arm swinging and landing from jumps are the most common causes of volleyball injuries.

CHAPTER 7

Courting Disaster

With all the jumping, arm swinging, diving, and other quick moves volleyball players make, it is not surprising that injuries occur. The organization Stop Sports Injuries says, "While volleyball injuries rank lowest for all major sports, volleyball players are at risk for both traumatic and overuse injuries."[55] Traumatic injuries come from sudden trauma, such as falling down and breaking a bone, while overuse injuries develop gradually from repeated use of certain joints and muscles. The American Academy of Orthopaedic Surgeons (AAOS) reports that emergency rooms in the United States treated over fifty-eight thousand volleyball-related injuries of all types in 2010.

Sports Medicine

Sports medicine is the scientific field that deals with preventing, diagnosing, and treating sports injuries. While different types of medical doctors can practice sports medicine, most who do are sports medicine specialists. This means they complete extra training in sports medicine after they obtain their medical degree. Many also have a specialty in orthopaedic surgery, which means they specialize in operating on and otherwise treating bone and muscle injuries. Sports medicine physicians work closely with trainers, sports psychologists, nutritionists, and physical therapists and other rehabilitation therapists to help

Knee pads, ankle braces, and custom shoes are among the equipment worn by volleyball players at the University of Oregon during an NCAA championship tournament match.

athletes prevent injuries and get back on their feet after being injured.

Because many sports injuries are very painful and can derail athletic careers and team dynamics, sports medicine specialists emphasize injury prevention. The AAOS points out that many volleyball injuries can be prevented by using knee and elbow pads, ankle braces, and proper shoes and adequately warming up and cooling down muscles before and after practices and games. Good nutrition, adequate sleep, and overall body fitness can also help with injury prevention.

However, despite preventive measures, injuries that range from mild to severe do occur. While some injuries, such as mild muscle strains or bruises, do not take long to heal, others can take many months. Injuries that need surgery often require months of recovery and extensive rehabilitation to regain strength and other abilities. Some injuries are so severe that they result in permanent disability. For example, Kirk Kilgour, who played college and professional volleyball in the 1960s and 1970s, became a quadriplegic after suffering a back injury.

For those injuries that do heal, sports doctors say that a player's mental attitude and will to play again, along with his age and overall physical condition, strongly influence how quickly he recovers and gets back into shape. Volleyball champion Karch Kiraly is an example of an athlete who bounced back repeatedly from knee and shoulder injuries

No Doping Allowed

Besides addressing athletic injuries, sports medicine also deals with the illegal use of performance-enhancing drugs and medical procedures, also known as doping. Blood transfusions to increase blood oxygen levels; muscle-building drugs, such as steroids; and stimulant drugs, such as amphetamines are all banned by all amateur and professional sports agencies but continue to be used by some athletes at all levels of competition. All have serious side effects, and these dangers, along with the unfair advantages they may give athletes, have led the World Anti-Doping Agency (WADA), in conjunction with agencies such as Fédération Internationale de Volleyball (FIVB) and USA Volleyball, to implement screening rules and procedures. Local, national, and international rules mandate expulsion of athletes who violate doping rules or who refuse to be tested.

In encouraging athletes to comply with antidoping regulations, WADA states, "All medications have side effects—but taking them when your body doesn't need them can cause serious damage to your body and destroy your athletic career."

World Anti-Doping Agency. *Dangers of Doping: Get the Facts*. Brochure. World Anti-Doping Agency. www.fivb.org/EN/Medical/Document/WADA_Dangers_of_Doping_Leaflet_EN.pdf.

and surgeries during his more than thirty years in competitive volleyball. His wife, Janna, says she was amazed by how much her husband's mental strength pushed him to recover and keep competing. "I didn't think it was physically possible. It might have been after his first shoulder surgery, he didn't come back that quickly and he didn't look as strong. But as soon as you think that, he recovers and has a string of wins. It was amazing to see some of the things he did on sheer will and brains,"[56] she says.

The Most Common Volleyball Injury

Like Kiraly, many other volleyball players sustain shoulder and knee injuries. However, these are not the most common volleyball injuries. The number-one injury is ankle sprains. A sprain is a traumatic injury that involves overstretching and tearing ligaments that link muscles to bone. Similar injuries called strains involve overstretching and tearing a

PAINFUL INJURIES

The three most commonly injured areas for volleyball players are the shoulders, knees, and ankles. Injuries can result from overuse or acute trauma, and normally affect the ligaments and tendons connecting bone to bone, or muscle to bone.

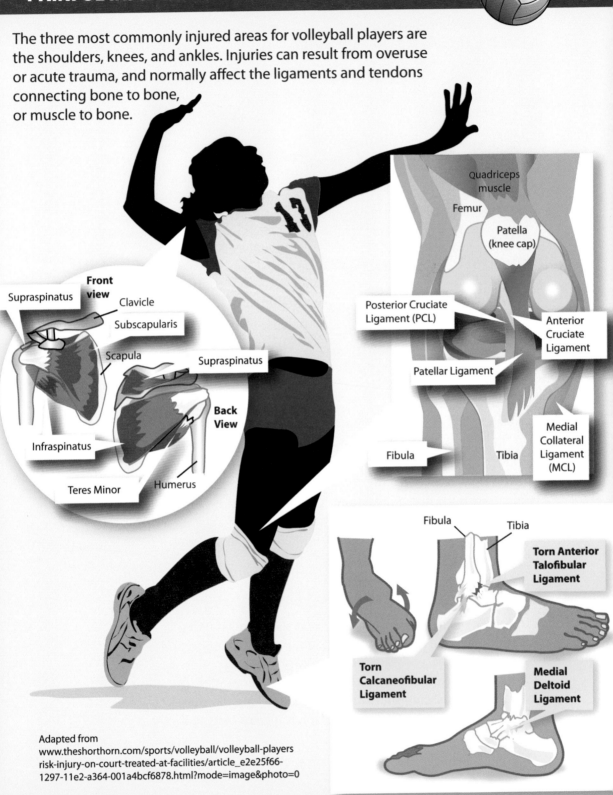

Front view

Supraspinatus
Clavicle
Subscapularis
Scapula
Supraspinatus
Infraspinatus
Teres Minor
Humerus

Back View

Quadriceps muscle
Femur
Patella (knee cap)
Posterior Cruciate Ligament (PCL)
Anterior Cruciate Ligament
Patellar Ligament
Medial Collateral Ligament (MCL)
Fibula
Tibia

Fibula
Tibia
Torn Anterior Talofibular Ligament
Torn Calcaneofibular Ligament
Medial Deltoid Ligament

muscle itself. Most of the time, ankle sprains and strains occur when landing from a jump or result from a rapid change of direction that makes the foot turn sideways.

Any of the four main ligaments around the four main anklebones can be affected by a sprain. Two of these bones, the tibia and fibula, are the long bones that constitute the shin. The other two bones are the talus, which fits into a socket formed by the bases of the tibia and fibula, and the calcaneus, commonly called the heel bone, which supports the talus. The most common type of ankle sprain in volleyball players involves damage to the talo-fibula ligament.

These sprains can range from mild to severe. A mild sprain comes from partial tearing of the ligament. Immediate treatment with rest, ice, elevation, and compression (bandaging to reduce swelling) usually leads to complete recovery within a few weeks. Severe sprains, in which the tissue is completely torn, may take many weeks to months to heal and may require surgery to repair the ligament. The leg may be unusable during healing, and sometimes the scar tissue that forms during healing leaves the ligament weakened or stiff.

Knee Trouble

Like ankle sprains, knee problems, the second most common volleyball injury, result from ground reaction forces putting stress on the joints and from overstretching and rotating the joints too quickly. While most ankle injuries are traumatic injuries, the most common knee injuries in volleyball result from repeated stresses due to overuse.

The most common knee injuries in volleyball players involve tears to the anterior cruciate ligament (ACL). *Anterior* means "front" and *cruciate* means "cross shaped." The ACL sits in front of the posterior cruciate ligament, and both form a cross that allows the knee to move forward or backward. These ligaments hold the femur (thigh) bone

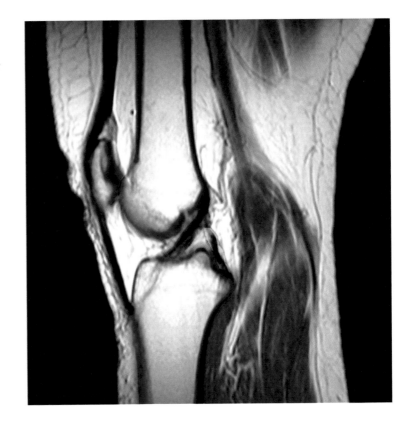

A color-enhanced sagittal MRI of a healthy human knee highlights the femur, tibia, and patella in blue, the anterior cruciate ligament (ACL) in orange, and the posterior cruciate ligament (PCL) in yellow. Volleyball players are prone to ACL injuries.

and tibia together. Although ACL injuries can result from a single trauma, in volleyball they most often result from repeated jump landings. These injuries are extremely painful and often require surgery to build a new ligament with tissue taken from another knee part. This surgery is more effective than simply sewing the ligament back together. Recovery and rehabilitation from the surgery, however, can be long and painful, and athletes dread ACL injuries. According to Manual A. Duarte in an article for the newsletter, *Dynamic Chiropractic,* "the athlete pays a high physical, mental, emotional and economic price for this severe injury."[57]

Because of the severity of ACL injuries, many studies evaluate the contributing factors. Several studies indicate that one way of reducing the chances of sustaining an ACL tear is to be sure to land from a jump on both feet rather than on just one. Athletes tend to flex their knees more during two-footed landings, and this decreases the ground reaction force and thus the stresses on the joints. A 2011 study

Rising Above a Disabling Injury

Some volleyball injuries not only derail sports careers but are also permanently disabling. Kirk Kilgour, who played volleyball for the University of California, Los Angeles, the U.S. National Team, and the Italian Professional League in the 1960s and 1970s, was seriously injured on January 8, 1976, during training. While performing agility drills, Kilgour fell and dislocated his spine, leaving him a quadriplegic.

Although his career as a player ended, Kilgour was determined to continue to contribute to volleyball. He served as assistant coach and worked his way up to head volleyball coach at Pepperdine University from 1977 to 1985. He then became a sports broadcaster, delivering commentary on volleyball in the 1984, 1992, and 1996 Olympics for news networks and covering many collegiate and professional volleyball matches.

Along with his stints in coaching and broadcasting, Kilgour worked as a tireless advocate for the disabled in the Los Angeles area until his death in 2002. He was instrumental in raising awareness of and implementing public policies that addressed disabled athletes' needs and mandated improved public facilities for wheelchair users.

explains how these factors interact: "The single-leg stop-jump produced a greater vertical ground reaction force than the double-leg stop-jump, which was likely due to the smaller hip and knee flexion angles at initial foot contact with the ground, the smaller maximum hip and knee flexion angles during landing, and the smaller knee flexion angular velocity at the time of initial foot contact with the ground."[58]

One reason greater ground reaction forces during jump landings result in greater stresses on the knees is that due to Newton's third law of motion, these forces are counteracted by greater muscle forces in the quadriceps muscles in the thighs. These muscle forces press down on the knee muscles, forcing them to straighten, which puts more strain on all parts of the knee than flexed muscles do.

Gender and ACL Injuries

Other studies found that female athletes in all sports sustain more ACL injuries than male athletes do, and sports medicine doctors have uncovered several possible reasons

A beach volleyball player from China receives medical treatment after injuring her knee during a match. Female athletes are more prone to ACL injuries than their male counterparts.

The Right Shoes

One factor that influences how volleyball players interact with the forces of physics is their shoes. The right shoes help absorb the impact of increased ground reaction forces during running and jumping, and thus reduce the chances of hip, back, leg, and foot injuries. The right shoes also provide the best traction to help players maintain their balance.

Early volleyball players generally wore tennis shoes. In 1952 the Japanese company ASICS invented the first volleyball shoes. Known as the Tiger, the shoes were lightweight with good traction to help with running and jumping. In 1957 ASICS introduced two slightly different models of the Tiger, one for offense and one for defense. Today there are many styles and brands of volleyball shoes designed for different skill specialties and different sized players.

for these findings. One factor that seems to play a role is the female hormone estrogen. Female athletes experience the greatest number of ACL injuries right before they begin menstruating, when estrogen levels are high, suggesting that estrogen may be at least partly responsible. No one, however, knows how or why estrogen may affect ligaments.

Other researchers found gender differences in the biomechanics of jump landings. Scientists at Swansea University in Wales measured knee flexion in males and females performing volleyball blocking jumps and found that females flex their knees a great deal less than males do when landing. Females also have greater angular velocity in their knees when landing from a jump. This finding led the researchers to conclude that "the results appear to indicate less dynamic [motion-related] stability of the knee during landing in females compared to males which may be a contributory factor in the reported greater incidence of ACL injury in females."[59] To address these factors, the researchers suggest that female athletes spend more time doing strength-training exercises that increase knee stability. Although ligaments cannot be strengthened, muscles can, and this can help stabilize joints.

Another contributing factor is that female athletes have more flexible hamstring muscles than males do, and this makes it more difficult for them to flex their knees during jump landings. This finding led experts to encourage females to perform more strength-training exercises for the hamstrings. While the quadriceps muscles on the front of the thighs control knee extension, the hamstrings on the back of the thighs control knee flexion. Flexibility in the hamstrings is very desirable for avoiding some injuries, but very flexible muscles tend to be weaker than less flexible ones. Sports doctors suggest that balancing flexibility and strength-training exercises can help resolve this problem.

Shouldering the Burden

Proper training and conditioning exercises can also help reduce the risk of shoulder injuries, the third most common type of volleyball injury. Many players develop shoulder

A Brazilian player extends his arm and shoulder to spike the ball over the net. The torque and rotation velocity created by the overhead arm motion of a spike can cause shoulder injuries.

cuff muscles furnish much of the power for overhead moves in volleyball, it is not surprising that overuse often results in an injury called rotator cuff tendinopathy. Here, the tendons that bind these muscles to bones can become inflamed, leading to increasingly severe pain. The tendons can also tear, leading to sudden, sharp pain. Ice, heat, and medication to lessen inflammation are often effective treatments, but sometimes surgery is needed to repair torn tissue.

An even more common overuse injury known as infraspinatus syndrome (IS), or volleyball shoulder, is often painless until extensive damage is done to the infraspinatus muscle. Infraspinatus syndrome is caused by suprascapular neuropathy, which involves degeneration in the nerve that runs along the top of the suprascapular muscle. Sometimes IS is misdiagnosed as rotator cuff tendinopathy, but magnetic resonance imaging (MRI) tests can distinguish the two conditions by identifying the muscle injuries and nerve abnormalities that underlie IS. The suprascapular nerve provides input from the brain and spinal cord to the suprascapular and infraspinatus muscles. Frequent pressure on this nerve from overhead motions can cause the nerve to fall apart, and this in turn leads to atrophy (wasting) and weakness in these muscles, particularly in the infraspinatus muscle. It is estimated that between 13 and 45 percent of elite volleyball players have suprascapular neuropathy.

Athletes in all sports that require repeated overhead motions are at risk for IS, but a 2011 study found that "for reasons that are poorly understood, volleyball players are at greater risk of developing IS than are athletes who compete in other overhead sports."[62] By measuring joint and muscle activity in athletes playing tennis, baseball, and volleyball, the researchers in this study discovered that although the overhead motions are similar, volleyball spikes and serves involve greater shoulder abduction and horizontal adduction, which may explain the greater risk. Other biomechanical studies hypothesize that the repeated changes of direction of the infraspinatus muscle during the slowing-down phase of float serves may be responsible for the increased risk of IS, but this has not been proven.

Most cases of IS improve with treatment, which may include medication to decrease pain and inflammation, heat to relax muscles and increase blood flow to the area, exercises to strengthen the shoulder muscles and improve their range of motion, or surgery to relieve pressure on the supra-scapular nerve. Doctors say the sooner treatment is started, the better the outcome. Therefore, they suggest not waiting until the pain becomes unbearable to begin treatment.

Beach Volleyball Risks

Besides these most common injuries and other injuries to the back and hands that can affect all volleyball players, beach players also face possible heat cramps, heat exhaustion, or

A thermometer in the sand on a beach volleyball court at the 1996 Olympic Games registers a temperature of 120 degrees Fahrenheit. Beach volleyball players can run the risk of heat-related illness and injury.

heatstroke when playing in hot weather. With heat cramps, the athlete develops painful muscle spasms. In heat exhaustion, people become thirsty, weak, lightheaded, and nauseated, and they sweat profusely. The skin becomes clammy and the heart rate elevates, but the body temperature remains normal. In heatstroke, however, the body temperature rises rapidly, leading to confusion; bizarre behavior; fainting; dry, flushed skin; and lack of sweating. Heatstroke is a life-threatening emergency that will rapidly lead to coma and death without treatment to lower the body temperature. This may involve placing the person in an ice bath.

Athletes are usually careful to drink enough fluids to prevent heat-related emergencies, but they can still happen. Today people are more aware of the risks of overheating and take many precautions, but in beach tournaments back in the 1960s and 1970s, these problems, especially heat cramps, occurred fairly frequently. As Byron Shewman explains in his book, *Volleyball Centennial*,

> tournaments in those days were two days of many hours under a July sun for two guys covering 30 feet by 30 feet of hot, deep sand. Sweating, lunging, jumping, and more sweating, always sweating. Cramps were often a result. No matter how much liquid, salt and electrolytes [chemicals in sports drinks] were absorbed, a few players simply couldn't stave off the rapid dehydration and if any player ever witnessed a guy with full body cramps, he'd never forget it."[63]

People with full body cramps experience horrific pain and an inability to move their muscles. Only muscle-relaxing medications administered by a doctor can relieve this condition.

Today amateur and professional sports organizations use measurements of heat stress to warn athletes of dangerous conditions so they will take extra precautions or even cancel a match in overly hot weather. One widely used measurement is the Wet Bulb Globe Temperature, which incorporates temperature, humidity, wind speed, and solar radiation readings into a heat stress score that predicts the risk of heat-related illness. Despite such tools, players still occasionally develop these illnesses. In 2007 during the Fédération Internationale de Volleyball Grand Slam in Berlin, Germany, for instance, German beach volleyball player Eric Koreng experienced heat exhaustion so severe that his team forfeited the match.

Despite the reality that emergencies and injuries do occur, the fact that volleyball is safer than other competitive sports accounts for some of its widespread popularity among players at all levels of competition. The 800 million people worldwide who play volleyball welcome the lower risk of injury, and they also validate William Morgan's vision of creating a game that people of all ages could participate in for exercise and recreational enjoyment.

NOTES

Chapter 1: A Wildly Popular Sport

1. Team USA. "USA Volleyball: About Us." Team USA. www.teamusa.org/USA-Volleyball/About-Us.aspx.
2. Quoted in Harold Arthur Harris. *Sport in Greece and Rome.* Ithaca, NY: Cornell University Press, 1972, p. 82.
3. Quoted in Volleyball Coaching and Education Services. "The Volleyball Story." Volleyball Coaching and Education Services. www.volleyballces.com/vball_history.html.
4. Bonnie Kenny and Cindy Gregory. *Volleyball: Steps to Success.* Champaign, IL: Human Kinetics, 2006, p. ix.
5. Byron Shewman. *Volleyball Centennial.* Indianapolis, IN: Masters Press, 1995, p. 8.
6. Quoted in Volleyball World Wide. "Rally Scoring." Volleyball World Wide. www.volleyball.org/rules/rallyscoring.html.
7. Volleyball Hall of Fame. "Armed Forces of the United States." Volleyball Hall of Fame. www.volleyhall.org/usaf.html.
8. Volleyball Hall of Fame. "1984 U.S. Men's Olympic Team." Volleyball Hall of Fame. www.volleyhall.org/84Mens.html.
9. Quoted in Arthur R. Couvillon, *Sands of Time: The History of Beach Volleyball.* 3 vols. Hermosa Beach, CA: Information Guides, 2002–2004. Beach Volleyball Database. www.bvbinfo.com/SandsSneak.asp?issue=16.

Chapter 2: Physics and Volleyball

10. Topend Sports. "Sports Biomechanics: Physics of Sport." Topend Sports. www.topendsports.com/biomechanics/physics.htm.
11. Miriam N. Satern. "Defining the 'Correct Form:' Using Biomechanics to Develop Reliable and Valid Assessment Instruments." *Strategies: A Journal for Physical and Sport Educators,* November–December 2011, p. 32.
12. A.G. Moody. "Newton's Three Laws of Motion for Volleyball." LiveStrong.com, June 14, 2011. www.livestrong.com/article/442422-newtons-three-laws-of-motion-for-volleyball.
13. Quoted in Satya Shanmugham. "Meet Four Sporty Scientists."

Brookhaven National Laboratory, April 11, 2009. www.bnl.gov/today/story.asp?ITEM_NO=1000.

14. Strength and Power for Volleyball.com. "Volleyball Approaches." Strength and Power for Volleyball.com. www.strength-and-power-for-volleyball.com/volleyball-approaches.html.

15. Quoted in Irene Garcia. "Karch Kiraly Shows He Has Not Lost Winning Touch." *Los Angeles Times*, July 7, 1991. http://articles.latimes.com/1991-07-07/sports/sp-2962_1_Karch-Kiraly.

16. Dan Lithio and Eric Webb. "Optimizing a Volleyball Serve." Hope College Mathematics REU, October 14, 2006, p. 11. www.rose-hulman.edu/mathjournal/archives/2006/vol7-n2/paper11/v7n2-11pd.pdf.

17. Quoted in Rabindra D. Mehta and Jani Macari Pallis. "Sports Ball Aerodynamics: Effects of Velocity, Spin and Surface Roughness." *Materials and Science in Sports*, 2001, p. 197.

18. Brian Lewis. "Jump Start: Six Secrets to a Killer Jump Serve." *Volleyball Magazine*, January 1, 2006. www.volleyballmag.com/articles/118-jump-start-six-secrets-to-a-killer-jump-serve.

20. Jason R. Karp. "A Primer on Muscles." Idea Health & Fitness Association. www.ideafit.com/fitness-library/a-primer-on-muscles.

21. Robert J. Reber and Donald K. Layman. "Sports & Nutrition: The Winning Connection." University of Illinois Extension. http://urbanext.illinois.edu/hsnut/hsathletes3.html.

22. UCLA Physics & Astronomy K-6 Connection. "Applying Forces, Doing Work, and Developing Power." UCLA Physics & Astronomy K-6 Connection. www.physics.ucla.edu/k-6connection/forwpsa.htm.

23. National Council on Strength & Fitness. "How Does Velocity Affect Force and Power." National Council on Strength & Fitness. www.ncsf.org/enew/articles/articles-velocity-andpower.aspx.

24. National Council on Strength & Fitness. "How Does Velocity Affect Force and Power."

25. Michael H. Stone et al. "Maximum Strength-Power-Performance Relationships in Collegiate Throwers." *Journal of Strength and Conditioning Research* 17, no. 4 (2003): 740.

Chapter 3: Physical Training

19. Jason R. Karp. "Muscle Fiber Types and Training." CoachR.org. www.coachr.org/fiber.htm.

Chapter 4: Psychology and Volleyball

26. Cecile Reynaud. *Coaching Volleyball Technical and Tactical Skills*. Champaign, IL: Human Kinetics, 2011, p. 15.

27. Quoted in Mike Miazga. "All Hail the King." *Volleyball Magazine*, December 2007, p. 29.

28. Quoted in Nicole Auerbach. "USA's Kerri Walsh, Misty May-Treanor Want Golden Olympic End." *USA Today*, August 7, 2012. www .usatoday.com/sports/olympics/ london/volleyball/story/2012- 08-07/misty-may-treanor-kerri- walsh-medal/56852686/1.

29. Quoted in eHow. "How to Run a Cross Play in Volleyball." eHow. www.ehow.com/how_17306_run- cross-play.html.

30. Quoted in Jon Ackerman. "Misty May-Treanor, Kerri Walsh Jen- nings Enter Attack Mode." NBC News, August 5, 2012. www .nbcolympics.com/news-blogs/ blog=olympic-talk/post/may- treanor-walsh-jennings-enter -attack-mode.html?chrcontext=top- nbc-moments.

31. Volleyball Hall of Fame. "Karch Kiraly." Volleyball Hall of Fame. www.volleyhall.org/kiraly.html.

32. Quoted in Shewman. *Volleyball Centennial*, p. 180.

33. Quoted in Mike Miazga. "Al Scates Retires." *Volleyball Magazine*, May 3, 2012. www.volleyballmag.com/arti- cles/42680-al-scates-retires.

34. Volleyball Hall of Fame. "Karch Kiraly."

35. Teen Champion Mindset. "Mental Toughness Secrets." Teen Cham- pion Mindset. www.mentaltough nesstrainer.com/mental-tough- ness-secrets.

36. Jacob Freedman. "Trojans Bring Out Their Brooms Against North- ridge." *Daily Trojan*, April 22, 2012. http://dailytrojan.com/2012/04/22/ trojans-bring-out-their-brooms- against-northridge.

37. Edward Spooner. *The Science of Volleyball Practice Development and Drill Design*. Bloomington, IN: iUniverse, 2012, p. 21.

38. Quoted in Kelli Anderson. "Let Us Now Praise Karch Kiraly." SI.com, September 25, 2007. http://sportsil- lustrated.cnn.com/2007/more/09/25/ volleyball1001/index.html.

Chapter 5: The Biomechanics of Offense

39. K. Lee Lerner and Brenda Wilmoth Lerner. *World of Sports Science*. Farmington Hills, MI: Gale Group, 2007, p. 760.

40. Volleyball-Training-Ground.com. "With All of the Volleyball Posi- tions, Where Do You Belong on the Court?" Volleyball-Training- Ground.com. www.volleyball- training-ground.com/volleyball -positions.html.

41. Bonnie Kenny and Cindy Gregory. *Volleyball: Steps to Success*. Cham- paign, IL: Human Kinetics, 2006, p. 63.

42. Strength and Power for Volleyball. com. "Volleyball Skills." Strength and Power for Volleyball.com. www .strength-and-power-for-volley- ball.com/volleyball-skills-attack-hit .html.

43. Jeff Wanderer. "A Biomechanical Analysis of Three Blocking Footwork Patterns in Volleyball Players." Master's thesis, San Jose State University, 1996, pp. 14–15. http://scholarworks.sjsu.edu/cgi/viewcontent.cgi?article=2335&context=etd_theses&sei-redir=1&referrer.

44. Lin-Huan Hu, Yung Hsiang Chen, and Chenfu Huang. "A 3D Analysis of the Volleyball Spike." International Symposium on Biomechanics in Sports, 2005. http://w4.ub.uni-konstanz.de/cpa/article/viewFile/776/699.

45. Baxter Holmes. "Gene Selznick Dies at 82: Beach Volleyball Player Pioneered Sport in Southern California." *Los Angeles Times*, June 12, 2012. http://articles.latimes.com/2012/jun/12/local/la-me-gene-selznick-20120612.

46. Reynaud. *Coaching Volleyball Technical and Tactical Skills*, p. 24.

47. Marion Alexander and Adrian Honish. "An Analysis of the Volleyball Jump Serve." Coachesinfo.com. www.coachesinfo.com/index.php?option=com_content&view=article&id=10029;volleyball-spike-serve&catid=103;volleyball-generalarticles&Itemid=197.

48. Alexander and Honish, "An Analysis of the Volleyball Jump Serve."

49. Alexander and Honish, "An Analysis of the Volleyball Jump Serve."

Chapter 6: Digging into Defense

50. M.E. Ridgeway and N. Hamilton. "The Kinematics of Forearm Passing in Low Skilled and High Skilled Volleyball Players." In *Biomechanics in Sports V: Proceedings of the Fifth International Symposium of Biomechanics in Sports*, edited by L. Tsarouchas et al. Athens, Greece: Hellenic Sports Research Institute, Olympic Sports Center of Athens, p. 227.

51. Reynaud. *Coaching Volleyball Technical and Tactical Skills*, p. 56.

52. Quoted in LifeTips. "Player Tips." LifeTips. http://volleyball.lifetips.com/cat/58913/player-tips/index.html.

53. Reynaud. *Coaching Volleyball Technical and Tactical Skills*, p. 136.

54. Marion Alexander and Adrian Honish. "Footwork for the Volleyball Block." Sports Biomechanics Lab, University of Manitoba, Canada. http://umanitoba.ca/faculties/kinrec/research/media/footwork_block.pdf.

Chapter 7: Courting Disaster

55. Stop Sports Injuries. "Preventing Volleyball Injuries." Stop Sports Injuries. www.stopsportsinjuries.org/volleyball-injury-prevention.aspx.

56. Quoted in Mike Miazga. "All Hail the King," p. 29.

57. Manuel A. Duarte. "Anterior Cruciate Ligament Injuries in Female Athletes." *Dynamic Chiropractic*, November 18, 2008, p. 18.

58. Li-I Wang. "The Lower Extremity Biomechanics of Single-and Double-Leg Stop-Lump Tasks." *Journal of Sports Science and Medicine*, March 2011, p. 151.

59. Gerwyn Hughes, James Watkins, and Nick Owen. "The Effects of Opposition and Gender on Knee Kinematics and Ground Reaction Force During Landing from Volleyball Block Jumps." *Research Quarterly for Exercise and Sport* vol. 81, no. 4 (December 2010): p. 384.

60. Jonathan C. Reeser et al. "Upper Limb Biomechanics During the Volleyball Serve and Spike." *Sports Health: A Multidisciplinary Approach*, September–October 2010.

61. Reeser et al. "Upper Limb Biomechanics During the Volleyball Serve and Spike."

62. Jonathan C. Reeser, Glenn S. Fleisig, Anne M.J. Cools, Darcie Yount, Scott A. Magnus. "Biomechanical Insights into the Aetiology of Infraspinatus Syndrome." *British Journal of Sports Medicine*, 2011. http://bjsm.bmj.com/content/early/2012/04/25/bjsports-2011-090918.short?rss=1.

63. Shewman. *Volleyball Centennial*, p. 78.

ace: A serve that scores an immediate point because it cannot be returned.

agility: The ability to move quickly in any direction.

biomechanics: The study of how the laws of physics and mechanics affect how the body moves.

bump: A forearm pass.

dig: A defensive volleyball technique where the receiver gets under the ball to pass it.

dink: A tap or soft spike.

dive: A defensive move in which the player goes to the floor to rescue the ball.

flexion: How much a joint is bent.

inertia: The tendency of an object at rest to remain at rest.

kill: A ball that is hit into the opponents' court and cannot be returned.

kinesiology: The science of movement.

kinesthetic awareness: The ability of an individual to know where his body is in relation to his surroundings.

libero: A back-row defensive specialist in volleyball.

ligament: Cartilage that binds bones to each other.

mass: How much matter an object contains.

momentum: Mass times velocity; the tendency of a moving object to remain in motion unless stopped by a force.

plyometrics: Exercises that build muscle power.

proprioception: The ability of the nervous system to coordinate the body so it stays upright.

rally: Continuous game play across the net.

set: A two-handed overhead pass to a hitter.

spike: A hard-driving hit into the opponents' court.

sprain: Overstretching and tearing a ligament.

strain: Overstretching and tearing a muscle.

tendon: Cartilage that binds muscle to bone.

FOR MORE INFORMATION

Books

Gabrielle Vanderhoof. *Volleyball*. Broomall, PA: Mason Crest, 2010. This is a book for teens that discusses volleyball injuries, injury prevention, training, conditioning, and doping.

Internet Sources

Jenney Cheever. "How Are Volleyball and Physics Related." Life123. www.life123.com/parenting/education/physics/volleyball-and-physics.shtml. This article is a brief overview of the main concepts of physics that apply to volleyball.

Topend Sports. "Volleyball Physics." Topend Sports. www.topendsports.com/sport/volleyball/physics.htm. This article discusses some of the physics behind volleyball.

Natalie Woodhurst. "Volleyball & The Laws of Motion." Livestrong.com, May 26, 2011. www.livestrong.com/article/389715-volleyball-the-laws-of-motion. This article discusses how Newton's laws of motion relate to volleyball.

Brett Zarda. "Volleyball (On the Sand and In the Gym)." Popsci. www.popsci.com/know-your-olympic-sport/article/2008-08/volleyball-sand-and-gym. This article discusses some volleyball technology related to the 2008 Olympics.

INDEX

A

Acceleration, 26, 28, 29
Actin, 42
Adenosine triphosphate (ATP), 43–44
Aerobic exercise, 40, 44, 46
Agility, 47, 68, 71
Agonist, *39*
Air pressure, 34
Air resistance, 34
Alcinous, 9
Alexander, Marion, 79, 82, 92
American Academy of Orthopaedic
    Surgeons (AAOS), 95, 96
Amphetamines, 97
Anaerobic exercise, 43, 44, 46
Angular momentum, 75
Angular motion, 82
Angular velocity, 48, 103
Ankles, injuries to, *96, 97, 98*
Antagonist, *39*
Anterior cruciate ligament (ACL)
    gender and, *102,* 102–104
    injury to, 99–100, *100,* 105
ASICS, 103
Atrophy, 107

B

Badminton, 10
Balance, 68

Balance exercises, *46,* 48–49
Ballistics, 24, 50–51
Ball toss, 81
Barrel roll, 90, *91*
Baseball, 10–11
    knuckleball pitch in, 35
Basketball, 9, 79
Beach volleyball, 18–20, *19,* 79
    attire for, *54,* 61
    digging in, *87*
    ground reaction force in, 31
    injuries in, *102*
    legitimacy of, 20–21
    men's, 20
    movement of ball in, 36–37
    number of players on team, 19
    popularity of, 20
    risks in, *108,* 108–110
    sand in, *30,* 31
    size of courts, 13
    special effects in, 36–37
    sports psychology and, 54–55
    women's, 20
Beal, Doug, 50
Bernoulli, Daniel, 34
Bernoulli's principle, 34
Berzins, Aldis, 50
Biceps, *39,* 40
Bicycle kick, 90
Bikinis, 61

PICTURE CREDITS

ABOUT THE AUTHOR

Melissa Abramovitz holds a degree in psychology from the University of California, San Diego and has been a freelance writer for over twenty-five years. She has written hundreds of magazine articles for all age groups, from preschoolers through adults, along with more than thirty educational series books for children and teens, and numerous poems and short stories. Abramovitz is also the author of an acclaimed book for writers and several children's picture books. Much of her work is about science and health.